Learning GraphQL
Declarative Data Fetching for Modern Web Apps

Eve Porcello and Alex Banks

Beijing · Boston · Farnham · Sebastopol · Tokyo

Learning GraphQL

by Eve Porcello and Alex Banks

Published by O'Reilly Media, Inc., 1005 Gravenstein Highway North, Sebastopol, CA 95472.

O'Reilly books may be purchased for educational, business, or sales promotional use. Online editions are also available for most titles (*http://oreilly.com*). For more information, contact our corporate/institutional sales department: 800-998-9938 or *corporate@oreilly.com*.

Acquisitions Editor: Mary Treseler	**Indexer:** WordCo, Inc.
Development Editor: Alicia Young	**Interior Designer:** David Futato
Production Editor: Justin Billing	**Cover Designer:** Karen Montgomery
Copyeditor: Chris Edwards	**Illustrator:** Melanie Yarbrough
Proofreader: Octal Publishing, Inc.	

August 2018:   First Edition

Revision History for the First Edition
2018-08-08:   First Release
2019-02-08:   Second Release
2021-09-24:   Third Release

See *http://oreilly.com/catalog/errata.csp?isbn=9781492030713* for release details.

978-1-492-03071-3

[LSI]

Table of Contents

Preface. vii

1. Welcome to GraphQL. 1
   What Is GraphQL?   2
      The GraphQL Specification   4
      Design Principles of GraphQL   5
   Origins of GraphQL   5
   History of Data Transport   6
      Remote Procedure Call   6
      Simple Object Access Protocol   6
      REST   7
   REST Drawbacks   7
      Overfetching   8
      Underfetching   9
      Managing REST Endpoints   11
   GraphQL in the Real World   12
      GraphQL Clients   12

2. Graph Theory. 15
   Graph Theory Vocabulary   18
   History of Graph Theory   20
   Trees are Graphs   24
   Graphs in the Real World   27

3. The GraphQL Query Language. 31
   GraphQL API Tools   33
      GraphiQL   33
      GraphQL Playground   36

Public GraphQL APIs   38
The GraphQL Query   38
   Edges and Connections   41
   Fragments   43
Mutations   48
   Using Query Variables   50
Subscriptions   51
Introspection   52
Abstract Syntax Trees   53

4. Designing a Schema. **57**
Defining Types   57
   Types   58
   Scalar Types   59
   Enums   59
Connections and Lists   60
   One-to-One Connections   61
   One-to-Many Connections   62
   Many-to-Many Connections   64
   Lists of Different Types   66
Arguments   68
   Filtering Data   69
Mutations   72
Input Types   74
Return Types   77
Subscriptions   78
Schema Documentation   79

5. Creating a GraphQL API. **83**
Project Setup   83
Resolvers   84
   Root Resolvers   86
   Type Resolvers   88
   Using Inputs and Enums   91
   Edges and Connections   93
   Custom Scalars   97
apollo-server-express   102
Context   104
   Installing Mongo   104
   Adding Database to Context   105
GitHub Authorization   107
   Setting Up GitHub OAuth   108

The Authorization Process   111
githubAuth Mutation   112
Authenticating Users   115
Conclusion   121

6. **GraphQL Clients.** **123**
Using a GraphQL API   123
fetch Requests   123
graphql-request   125
Apollo Client   128
Apollo Client with React   128
Project Setup   129
Configure Apollo Client   129
The Query Component   131
The Mutation Component   135
Authorization   137
Authorizing the User   137
Identifying the User   141
Working with the Cache   143
Fetch Policies   143
Persisting The Cache   144
Updating the Cache   145

7. **GraphQL in the Real World.** **149**
Subscriptions   150
Working with Subscriptions   150
Consuming Subscriptions   156
Uploading Files   160
Handling Uploads on the Server   160
Posting a New Photo with Apollo Client   162
Security   168
Request Timeouts   169
Data Limitations   169
Limiting Query Depth   170
Limiting Query Complexity   172
Apollo Engine   174
Taking the Next Steps   175
Incremental Migration   175
Schema-First Development   176
GraphQL Events   178
Community   179
Community Slack Channels   180

Index. 181

Preface

Acknowledgments

This book would not be a book without the help of many phenomenal people. It started with the idea from Ally MacDonald, our editor for *Learning React*, who encouraged us to write *Learning GraphQL*. We were then very lucky to get to work with Alicia Young, who shepherded the book to its printing. Thanks to Justin Billing, Melanie Yarbrough, and Chris Edwards who sanded off all of the rough edges during an extremely thorough production edit.

Throughout the process, we were fortunate to get feedback from Peggy Rayzis and Sashko Stubailo from the Apollo team who shared their insights and hot tips about the latest features. Thanks also to Adam Rackis, Garrett McCullough, and Shivi Singh, who were excellent technical editors.

We wrote this book about GraphQL because we love GraphQL. We think you will too.

Conventions Used in This Book

The following typographical conventions are used in this book:

Italic
> Indicates new terms, URLs, email addresses, filenames, and file extensions.

`Constant width`
> Used for program listings, as well as within paragraphs to refer to program elements such as variable or function names, databases, data types, environment variables, statements, and keywords.

`Constant width bold`
> Shows commands or other text that should be typed literally by the user.

Constant width italic

> Shows text that should be replaced with user-supplied values or by values determined by context.

 This element signifies a tip or suggestion.

 This element signifies a general note.

 This element indicates a warning or caution.

Using Code Examples

Supplemental material (code examples, exercises, etc.) is available for download at *https://github.com/moonhighway/learning-graphql/*.

This book is here to help you get your job done. In general, if example code is offered with this book, you may use it in your programs and documentation. You do not need to contact us for permission unless you're reproducing a significant portion of the code. For example, writing a program that uses several chunks of code from this book does not require permission. Selling or distributing a CD-ROM of examples from O'Reilly books does require permission. Answering a question by citing this book and quoting example code does not require permission. Incorporating a significant amount of example code from this book into your product's documentation does require permission.

We appreciate, but do not require, attribution. An attribution usually includes the title, author, publisher, and ISBN. For example: "*Learning GraphQL* by Eve Porcello and Alex Banks (O'Reilly). Copyright 2018 Moon Highway, LLC, 978-1-492-03071-3."

If you feel your use of code examples falls outside fair use or the permission given above, feel free to contact us at *permissions@oreilly.com*.

O'Reilly Safari

 *Safari* (formerly Safari Books Online) is a membership-based training and reference platform for enterprise, government, educators, and individuals.

Members have access to thousands of books, training videos, Learning Paths, interactive tutorials, and curated playlists from over 250 publishers, including O'Reilly Media, Harvard Business Review, Prentice Hall Professional, Addison-Wesley Professional, Microsoft Press, Sams, Que, Peachpit Press, Adobe, Focal Press, Cisco Press, John Wiley & Sons, Syngress, Morgan Kaufmann, IBM Redbooks, Packt, Adobe Press, FT Press, Apress, Manning, New Riders, McGraw-Hill, Jones & Bartlett, and Course Technology, among others.

For more information, please visit *http://oreilly.com/safari*.

How to Contact Us

Please address comments and questions concerning this book to the publisher:

> O'Reilly Media, Inc.
> 1005 Gravenstein Highway North
> Sebastopol, CA 95472
> 800-998-9938 (in the United States or Canada)
> 707-829-0515 (international or local)
> 707-829-0104 (fax)

We have a web page for this book where we list errata and any additional information. You can access this page at *http://bit.ly/learning-graphql-orm*.

To comment or ask technical questions about this book, send email to *bookquestions@oreilly.com*.

For more information about our books, courses, conferences, and news, see our website at http://www.oreilly.com.

Find us on Facebook: http://facebook.com/oreilly

Follow us on Twitter: http://twitter.com/oreillymedia

Watch us on YouTube: http://www.youtube.com/oreillymedia

CHAPTER 1
Welcome to GraphQL

Before the Queen of England made him a knight, Tim Berners-Lee was a programmer. He worked at CERN, the European particle physics laboratory in Switzerland, and was surrounded by a swath of talented researchers. Berners-Lee wanted to help his colleagues share their ideas, so he decided to create a network in which scientists could post and update information. The project eventually became the first web server and the first web client, and the "WorldWideWeb" browser (later renamed "Nexus") was rolled out at CERN (*https://www.w3.org/People/Berners-Lee/ Longer.html*) in December 1990.

With his project, Berners-Lee made it possible for researchers to view and update web content on their own computers. "WorldWideWeb" was HTML, URLs, a browser, and a WYSIWYG interface in which to update content.

Today, the internet isn't just HTML in a browser. The internet is laptops. It's wrist watches. It's smartphones. It's a radio-frequency identification (RFID) chip in your ski lift ticket. It's a robot that feeds your cat treats while you're out of town.

The clients are more numerous today, but we're still striving to do the same thing: load data somewhere as fast as possible. We need our applications to be performant because our users hold us to a high standard. They expect our apps to work well under any condition: from 2G on feature phones to blazing-fast fiber internet on big-screen desktop computers. Fast apps make it easier for more people to interact with our content. Fast apps make our users happy. And, yes, fast apps make us money.

Getting data from a server to the client quickly and predictably is the story of the web, past, present, and future. Although this book will often dig in to the past for context, we're here to talk about modern solutions. We're here to talk about the future. We're here to talk about GraphQL.

What Is GraphQL?

GraphQL (*https://www.graphql.org/*) is a query language for your APIs. It's also a run-time for fulfilling queries with your data. The GraphQL service is transport agnostic but is typically served over HTTP.

To demonstrate a GraphQL query and its response, let's take a look at SWAPI (*https://graphql.org/swapi-graphql/*), the Star Wars API. SWAPI is a Representational State Transfer (REST) API that has been wrapped with GraphQL. We can use it to send queries and receive data.

A GraphQL query asks only for the data that it needs. Figure 1-1 is an example of a GraphQL query. The query is on the left. We request the data for a person, Princess Leia. We obtain Leia Organa's record because we specify that we want the fifth person (`personID:5`). Next, we ask for three fields of data: `name`, `birthYear`, and `created`. On the right is our response: JSON data formatted to match the shape of our query. This response contains only the data that we need.

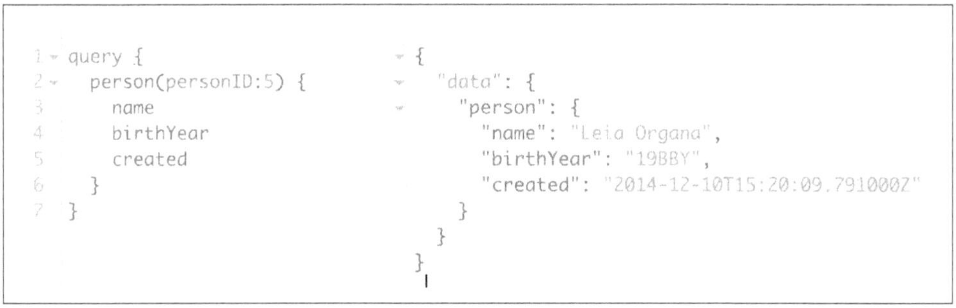

```
1 ▾ query {                          ▾ {
2 ▾   person(personID:5) {             ▾ "data": {
3       name                           ▾ "person": {
4       birthYear                          "name": "Leia Organa",
5       created                            "birthYear": "19BBY",
6     }                                    "created": "2014-12-10T15:20:09.791000Z"
7   }                                    }
                                       }
                                     }
```

Figure 1-1. Person query for the Star Wars API

We can then adjust the query because queries are interactive. We can change it and see a new result. If we add the field `filmConnection`, we can request the title of each of Leia's films, as Figure 1-2 shows.

```
1 ▾ query {                              ▾ {
2 ▾   person(personID:5) {              ▾     "data": {
3         name                                "person": {
4         birthYear                             "name": "Leia Organa",
5         created                               "birthYear": "19BBY",
6 ▾       filmConnection {                      "created": "2014-12-10T15:20:09.791000Z",
7           films {                     ▾       "filmConnection": {
8             title                     ▾         "films": [
9           }                                       {
10        }                                           "title": "A New Hope"
11      }                                           },
12    }                                             {
                                                      "title": "The Empire Strikes Back"
                                                    },
                                                    {
                                                      "title": "Return of the Jedi"
                                                    },
                                                    {
                                                      "title": "Revenge of the Sith"
                                                    },
                                                    {
                                                      "title": "The Force Awakens"
                                                    }
                                                  ]
                                                }
                                              }
                                            }
                                          }
```

Figure 1-2. Connection query

The query is nested, and when it is executed, can traverse related objects. This allows us to make one HTTP request for two types of data. We don't need to make several round trips to drill down into multiple objects. We don't receive additional unwanted data about those types. With GraphQL, our clients can obtain all of the data they need in one request.

Whenever a query is executed against a GraphQL server, it is validated against a type system. Every GraphQL service defines types in a GraphQL schema. You can think of a type system as a blueprint for your API's data, backed by a list of objects that you define. For example, the person query from earlier is backed by a Person object:

```
type Person {
    id: ID!
    name: String
    birthYear: String
    eyeColor: String
    gender: String
    hairColor: String
    height: Int
    mass: Float
    skinColor: String
    homeworld: Planet
    species: Species
```

```
    filmConnection: PersonFilmsConnection
    starshipConnection: PersonStarshipConnection
    vehicleConnection: PersonVehiclesConnection
    created: String
    edited: String
}
```

The `Person` type defines all of the fields, along with their types, that are available to query on Princess Leia. In Chapter 3, we dig deeper into the schema and GraphQL's type system.

GraphQL is often referred to as a *declarative* data-fetching language. By that, we mean that developers will list their data requirements as *what* data they need without focusing on *how* they're going to get it. GraphQL server libraries exist in a variety of different languages including C#, Clojure, Elixir, Erlang, Go, Groovy, Java, JavaScript, .NET, PHP, Python, Scala, and Ruby.[1]

In this book, we focus on how to build GraphQL services with JavaScript. All of the techniques that we discuss throughout this book are applicable to GraphQL in any language.

The GraphQL Specification

GraphQL is a specification (spec) for client-server communication. What is a spec? A spec describes the capabilities and characteristics of a language. We benefit from language specifications because they supply a common vocabulary and best practices for the community's use of the language.

A fairly notable example of a software spec is the ECMAScript spec. Every once in a while, a group of representatives from browser companies, tech companies, and the community at large get together and devise what should be included in (and left out of) the ECMAScript spec. The same is true for GraphQL. A group of individuals got together and wrote what should be included in (and left out of) the language. This serves as a guideline for all of the implementations of GraphQL.

When the spec was released, the creators of GraphQL also shared a reference implementation of a GraphQL server in JavaScript—graphql.js (*https://github.com/graphql/graphql-js*). This is useful as a blueprint, but the goal of this reference implementation is not to mandate which language you use to implement your service. It's merely a guide. After you have an understanding of the query language and the type system, you can build your server in any language you'd like.

If a spec and an implementation are different, what is actually in the spec? The spec describes the language and grammar you should use when writing queries. It also sets

---

1 See the GraphQL Server Libraries at *https://graphql.org/code/*.

up a type system plus the execution and validation engines of that type system. Beyond that, the spec isn't particularly bossy. GraphQL doesn't dictate which language to use, how the data should be stored, or which clients to support. The query language has guidelines but the actual design of your project is up to you. (If you'd like to dig into the whole thing, you can explore the documentation (*http://facebook.github.io/graphql/*).)

Design Principles of GraphQL

Even though GraphQL is not controlling about how you build your API, it does offer some guidelines for how to think about a service:[2]

Hierarchical
A GraphQL query is hierarchical. Fields are nested within other fields and the query is shaped like the data that it returns.

Product centric
GraphQL is driven by the data needs of the client and the language and runtime that support the client.

Strong typing
A GraphQL server is backed by the GraphQL type system. In the schema, each data point has a specific type against which it will be validated.

Client-specified queries
A GraphQL server provides the capabilities that the clients are allowed to consume.

Introspective
The GraphQL language is able to query the GraphQL server's type system.

Now that we have an introductory understanding of what the GraphQL spec is, let's look at why it was created.

Origins of GraphQL

In 2012, Facebook decided that it needed to rebuild the application's native mobile apps. The company's iOS and Android apps were just thin wrappers around the views of the mobile website. Facebook had a RESTful server and FQL (Facebook's version of SQL) data tables. Performance was struggling and the apps often crashed. At that

---

2 See the GraphQL Spec, June 2018 (*http://facebook.github.io/graphql/June2018/#sec-Overview*).

point, engineers realized they needed to improve the way that data was being sent to their client applications.[3]

The team of Lee Byron, Nick Schrock, and Dan Schafer decided to rethink their data from the client side. They set out to build GraphQL, a query language that would describe the capabilities and requirements of data models for the company's client/server applications.

In July 2015, the team released its initial GraphQL specification and a reference implementation of GraphQL in JavaScript called graphql.js. In September 2016, GraphQL left its "technical preview" stage. This meant that GraphQL was officially production-ready, even though it already had been used for years in production at Facebook. Today, GraphQL now powers almost all of Facebook's data fetching and is used in production by IBM, Intuit, Airbnb, and more.

History of Data Transport

GraphQL presents some very new ideas but all should be understood in a historical context of data transport. When we think about data transport, we're trying to make sense of how to pass data back and forth between computers. We request some data from a remote system and expect a response.

Remote Procedure Call

In the 1960s, remote procedure call (RPC) was invented. An RPC was initiated by the client, which sent a request message to a remote computer to do something. The remote computer sent a response to the client. These computers were different from clients and servers that we use today, but the flow of information was basically the same: request some data from the client, get a response from the server.

Simple Object Access Protocol

In the late 1990s, Simple Object Access Protocol (SOAP) emerged at Microsoft. SOAP used XML to encode a message and HTTP as a transport. SOAP also used a type system and introduced the concept of resource-oriented calls for data. SOAP offered fairly predictable results but caused frustration because SOAP implementations were fairly complicated.

---

3 See "Data Fetching for React Applications" by Dan Schafer and Jing Chen, *https://www.youtube.com/watch?v=9sc8Pyc51uU*.

REST

The API paradigm that you're probably most familiar with today is REST. REST was defined in 2000 in Roy Fielding's doctoral dissertation (*http://bit.ly/2j4SIKI*) at University of California–Irvine. He described a resource-oriented architecture in which users would progress through web resources by performing operations such as GET, PUT, POST, and DELETE. The network of resources can be thought of as a *virtual state machine*, and the actions (GET, PUT, POST, DELETE) are state changes within the machine. We might take it for granted today, but this was pretty huge. (Oh, and Fielding did get his Ph.D.)

In a RESTful architecture, routes represent information. For example, requesting information from each of these routes will yield a specific response:

```
/api/food/hot-dog
/api/sport/skiing
/api/city/Lisbon
```

REST allows us to create a data model with a variety of endpoints, a far simpler approach than previous architectures. It provided a new way to handle data on the increasingly complex web but didn't enforce a specific data response format. Initially, REST was used with XML. AJAX was originally an acronym that stood for Asynchronous JavaScript And XML, because the response data from an Ajax request was formatted as XML (it is now a freestanding word, spelled "Ajax"). This created a painful step for web developers: the need to parse XML responses before the data could be used in JavaScript.

Soon after, JavaScript Object Notation (JSON) was developed and standardized by Douglas Crockford. JSON is language agnostic and provides an elegant data format that many different languages can parse and consume. Crockford went on to write the seminal *JavaScript: The Good Parts* (*http://http://bit.ly/js-good-parts*) (O'Reilly, 2008) in which he let us know that JSON was one of the good parts.

The influence of REST is undeniable. It's used to build countless APIs. Developers up and down the stack have benefitted from it. There are even devotees so interested in arguing about what is and is not RESTful that they've been dubbed *RESTafarians*. So, if that's the case, why did Byron, Schrock, and Schafer embark on their journey to create something new? We can find the answer in some of REST's shortcomings.

REST Drawbacks

When GraphQL was first released, some touted it as a replacement to REST. "REST is dead!" early adopters cried, and then encouraged us all to throw a shovel in the trunk and drive our unsuspecting REST APIs out to the woods. This was great for getting clicks on blogs and starting conversations at conferences, but painting GraphQL as a REST killer is an oversimplification. A more nuanced take is that as the web has evolved, REST has shown signs of strain under certain conditions. GraphQL was built to ease the strain.

Overfetching

Suppose that we're building an app that uses data from the REST version of SWAPI. First, we need to load some data about character number 1, Luke Skywalker.[4] We can make a GET request for this information by visiting *https://swapi.co/api/people/1/*. The response is this JSON data:

```
{
  "name": "Luke Skywalker",
  "height": "172",
  "mass": "77",
  "hair_color": "blond",
  "skin_color": "fair",
  "eye_color": "blue",
  "birth_year": "19BBY",
  "gender": "male",
  "homeworld": "https://swapi.co/api/planets/1/",
  "films": [
    "https://swapi.co/api/films/2/",
    "https://swapi.co/api/films/6/",
    "https://swapi.co/api/films/3/",
    "https://swapi.co/api/films/1/",
    "https://swapi.co/api/films/7/"
  ],
  "species": [
    "https://swapi.co/api/species/1/"
  ],
  "vehicles": [
    "https://swapi.co/api/vehicles/14/",
    "https://swapi.co/api/vehicles/30/"
  ],
  "starships": [
    "https://swapi.co/api/starships/12/",
    "https://swapi.co/api/starships/22/"
  ],
  "created": "2014-12-09T13:50:51.644000Z",
  "edited": "2014-12-20T21:17:56.891000Z",
  "url": "https://swapi.co/api/people/1/"
}
```

This is a huge response. The response exceeds our app's data needs. We just need the information for name, mass, and height:

```
{
  "name": "Luke Skywalker",
```

---

4 Note that the SWAPI data doesn't include the most recent Star Wars films.

```
    "height": "172",
    "mass": "77"
}
```

This is a clear case of *overfetching*—we're getting a lot of data back that we don't need. The client requires three data points, but we're getting back an object with 16 keys and sending information over the network that is useless.

In a GraphQL application, how would this request look? We still want Luke Skywalker's name, height, and mass here in Figure 1-3.

```
query {                      ▼ {
  person(personID:1) {       ▼   "data": {
    name                     ▼     "person": {
    height                           "name": "Luke Skywalker",
    mass                             "height": 172,
  }                                  "mass": 77
}                                  }
                                 }
                               }
                             }
```

Figure 1-3. Luke Skywalker query

On the left, we issue our GraphQL query. We ask for only the fields that we want. On the right, we receive a JSON response, this time containing only the data that we requested, not 13 extra fields that are required to travel from a cell tower to a phone for no reason at all. We ask for data in a certain shape, we receive the data back in that shape. Nothing more, nothing less. This is more declarative and will likely yield a faster response given that extraneous data is not being fetched.

Underfetching

Our project manager just showed up at our desk and wants to add another feature to the Star Wars app. In addition to name, height, and mass, we now need to display a list of movie titles for all films that Luke Skywalker is in. After we request the data from *https://swapi.co/api/people/1/*, we still need to make additional requests for more data. This means we *underfetched*.

To get the title of each film, we need to fetch data from each of the routes in the films array:

```
"films": [
  "https://swapi.co/api/films/2/",
  "https://swapi.co/api/films/6/",
  "https://swapi.co/api/films/3/",
```

```
    "https://swapi.co/api/films/1/",
    "https://swapi.co/api/films/7/"
]
```

Getting this data requires one request for Luke Skywalker (`https://swapi.co/api/`
`people/1/`) and then five more for each of the films. For each film, we get another
large object. This time, we use only one value.

```
{
"title": "The Empire Strikes Back",
"episode_id": 5,
"opening_crawl": "...",
"director": "Irvin Kershner",
"producer": "Gary Kurtz, Rick McCallum",
"release_date": "1980-05-17",
"characters": [
  "https://swapi.co/api/people/1/",
  "https://swapi.co/api/people/2/",
  "https://swapi.co/api/people/3/",
  "https://swapi.co/api/people/4/",
  "https://swapi.co/api/people/5/",
  "https://swapi.co/api/people/10/",
  "https://swapi.co/api/people/13/",
  "https://swapi.co/api/people/14/",
  "https://swapi.co/api/people/18/",
  "https://swapi.co/api/people/20/",
  "https://swapi.co/api/people/21/",
  "https://swapi.co/api/people/22/",
  "https://swapi.co/api/people/23/",
  "https://swapi.co/api/people/24/",
  "https://swapi.co/api/people/25/",
  "https://swapi.co/api/people/26/"
],
"planets": [
      //... Long list of routes
  ],
"starships": [
      //... Long list of routes
  ],
"vehicles": [
      //... Long list of routes
  ],
"species": [
      //... Long list of routes
  ],
"created": "2014-12-12T11:26:24.656000Z",
"edited": "2017-04-19T10:57:29.544256Z",
"url": "https://swapi.co/api/films/2/"
}
```

If we wanted to list the characters that are part of this movie, we'd need to make a lot
more requests. In this case, we'd need to hit 16 more routes and make 16 more round-

trips to the client. Each HTTP request uses client resources and overfetches data. The result is a slower user experience, and users with slower network speeds or slower devices might not be able to view the content at all.

The GraphQL solution to underfetching is to define a nested query and then request the data all in one fetch, as Figure 1-4 shows.

```
 1 ▾ query {
 2 ▾   person(personID:1) {
 3       name
 4       height
 5       mass
 6 ▾     filmConnection {
 7         films {
 8           title
 9         }
10       }
11     }
12   }
```

```
 ▾ {
 ▾   "data": {
 ▾     "person": {
         "name": "Luke Skywalker",
         "height": 172,
         "mass": 77,
         "filmConnection": {
           "films": [
             {
               "title": "A New Hope"
             },
             {
               "title": "The Empire Strikes Back"
             },
             {
               "title": "Return of the Jedi"
             },
             {
               "title": "Revenge of the Sith"
             },
             {
               "title": "The Force Awakens"
             }
           ]
         }
       }
     }
   }
```

Figure 1-4. Films connection

Here, we receive only the data that we need in one request. And, as always, the shape of the query matches the shape of the returned data.

Managing REST Endpoints

Another common complaint about REST APIs is the lack of flexibility. As the needs on the client change, you usually have to create new endpoints, and those endpoints can begin to multiply quickly. To paraphrase Oprah, "You get a route! You get a route! Every! Body! Gets! A! Route!"

With the SWAPI REST API, we had to make requests to numerous routes. Larger apps typically utilize custom endpoints to minimize HTTP requests. You might see endpoints like /api/character-with-movie-title begin popping up. Development speed can be slow because setting up new endpoints often means that frontend and backend teams have more planning and communication to do with each other.

With GraphQL, the typical architecture involves a single endpoint. The single endpoint can act as a gateway and orchestrate several data sources, but the one endpoint still makes organization of data easier.

In this discussion of REST drawbacks, it's important to note that many organizations use GraphQL and REST together. Setting up a GraphQL endpoint that fetches data from REST endpoints is a perfectly valid way to use GraphQL. It can be a great way to incrementally adopt GraphQL at your organization.

GraphQL in the Real World

GraphQL is used by a variety of companies to power their apps, websites, and APIs. One of the most visible early adopters of GraphQL was GitHub. Its REST API went through three iterations, and version 4 of its public API uses GraphQL. As it mentions on the website (*https://developer.github.com/v4/*), GitHub found that "the ability to define precisely the data you want-and only the data you want-is a powerful advantage over the REST API v3 endpoints."

Other companies, like *The New York Times*, IBM, Twitter, and Yelp, have put their faith in GraphQL, as well, and developers from those teams are often found evangelizing the benefits of GraphQL at conferences.

There are at least three conferences devoted to GraphQL specifically: GraphQL Summit in San Francisco, GraphQL Finland in Helsinki, and GraphQL Europe in Berlin. The community continues to grow via local meetups and a variety of software conferences.

GraphQL Clients

As we've said numerous times, GraphQL is just a spec. It doesn't care whether you're using it with React or Vue or JavaScript or even a browser. GraphQL has opinions about a few specific topics, but beyond that, your architectural decisions are up to you. This has led to the emergence of tools to enforce some choices beyond the spec. Enter GraphQL clients.

GraphQL clients have emerged to speed the workflow for developer teams and improve the efficiency and performance of applications. They handle tasks like network requests, data caching, and injecting data into the user interface. There are many GraphQL clients, but the leaders in the space are Relay (*https://facebook.github.io/relay/*) and Apollo (*https://www.apollographql.com/*).

Relay is Facebook's client that works with React and React Native. Relay aims to be the connective tissue between React components and the data that is fetched from the GraphQL server. Relay is used by Facebook, GitHub, Twitch, and more.

Apollo Client was developed at Meteor Development Group and is a community-driven effort to build more comprehensive tooling around GraphQL. Apollo Client supports all major frontend development platforms and is framework agnostic. Apollo also develops tools that assist with the creation of GraphQL services, the performance enhancement of backend services, and tools to monitor the performance of GraphQL APIs. Companies, including Airbnb, CNBC, *The New York Times*, and Ticketmaster use Apollo Client in production.

The ecosystem is large and continues to change, but the good news is that the GraphQL spec is a pretty stable standard. In upcoming chapters, we discuss how to write a schema and create a GraphQL server. Along the way, there are learning resources to support your journey in this book's GitHub repository: *https://github.com/moonhighway/learning-graphql/*. There you'll find helpful links, samples, and all of the project files by chapter.

Before we dig in to the tactics of working with GraphQL, let's talk a bit about graph theory and the rich history of the ideas found in GraphQL.

CHAPTER 2
Graph Theory

The alarm sounds. You reach for your phone. When you turn off the beeping, you see two notifications. Fifteen people liked a tweet that you wrote last night. Nice. Three people retweeted it. Double nice. Your momentary Twitter notoriety was brought to you by a graph (as seen in Figure 2-1).

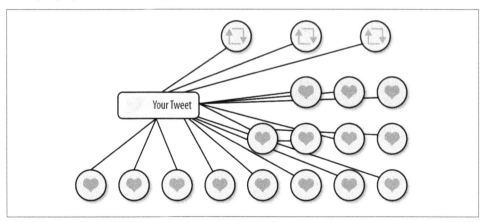

Figure 2-1. Twitter likes and retweets diagram

You're running up the stairs to catch the "L" at Irving Park. You jump in right before the doors close. Perfect. The train shakes side to side as you move forward, connecting every stop.

The doors open and close at each station. First, Addison. Then, Paulina, Southport, and Belmont. At Belmont, you cross the platform to transfer to the Red Line. On the Red Line, you make two more stops: Fullerton and North/Clybourn. This graph brought you to work, as shown in Figure 2-2.

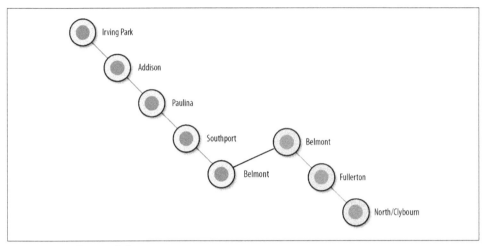

Figure 2-2. Chicago "L" map

You're riding the escalator up to street level when your phone rings. It's your sister. She says that she wants to buy train tickets to go to your Grandpa's 80th birthday party in July. "Mom's dad or Dad's dad?" you ask. "Dad's, but I think Mom's parents will be there, too. And Aunt Linda and Uncle Steve." You begin to picture who will be there. Another party planned by another graph: a family tree. Figure 2-3 shows this graph.

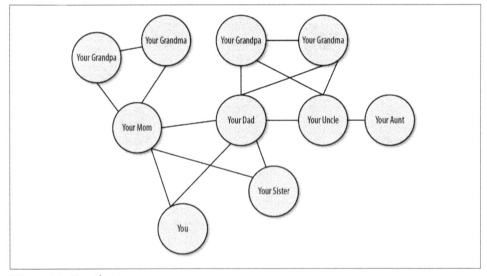

Figure 2-3. Family tree

Before long, you begin noticing graphs everywhere. You see them in social media apps, route maps, and snow day phone trees. And, from spectacular celestial constellations as seen in Figure 2-4.

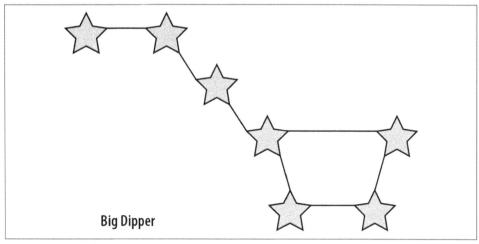

Figure 2-4. Big dipper

To nature's smallest building blocks, seen in Figure 2-5.

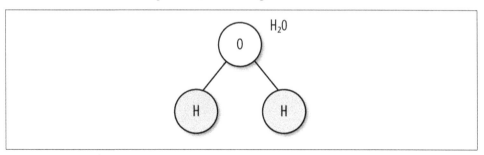

Figure 2-5. H_2O diagram

Graphs are all around us because they are a great way to diagram interconnected items, people, ideas, or pieces of data. But where did the concept of a graph come from? To understand this, we can take a closer look at *graph theory* and its origin in mathematics.

 You don't need to know anything about graph theory to work successfully with GraphQL. There won't be a quiz. We do, however, think it's interesting to explore the history behind these concepts to add some additional context.

Graph Theory Vocabulary

Graph theory is the study of graphs. Graphs are used formally to represent a collection of interconnected objects. You can think of a graph as an object containing data points and their connections. In computer science, graphs typically describe networks of data. A graph might look something like that shown in Figure 2-6.

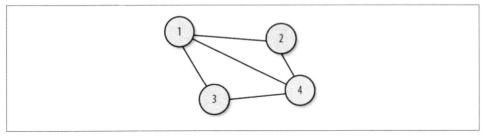

Figure 2-6. Graph diagram

This graph diagram is made up of four circles that represent data points. In graph terminology, these are called *nodes* or *vertices*. The lines or connections between these nodes are called *edges*, of which there are five.[1]

As an equation, a graph is $G = (V, E)$.

Starting from the easiest abbreviation, G stands for graph, and V describes a set of vertices or nodes. For this graph, V would equal the following:

```
vertices = { 1, 2, 3, 4}
```

E stands for a set of edges. Edges are represented by pairs of nodes.

```
edges = { {1, 2},
          {1, 3},
          {1, 4},
          {2, 4},
          {3, 4} }
```

In the list of edge pairs, what would happen if we rearranged their order? For example:

```
edges = { {4, 3},
          {4, 2},
          {4, 1},
          {3, 1},
          {2, 1} }
```

In this case, the graph remains the same, as Figure 2-7 shows.

---

1 For additional reading on nodes and edges, check out Vaidehi Joshi's blog post, "A Gentle Introduction to Graph Theory." (*https://dev.to/vaidehijoshi/a-gentle-introduction-to-graph-theory*)

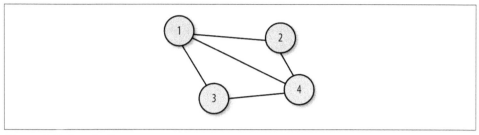

Figure 2-7. Graph diagram

The equation still represents the graph because there is no direction or hierarchy between the nodes. In graph theory, we call this an *undirected graph* (*https:// algs4.cs.princeton.edu/41graph/*). The edge definitions, or connections between data points, are *unordered pairs*.

When traversing, or visiting, different nodes of this graph, you could start anywhere and end anywhere, moving in any direction. Data doesn't follow in an obvious numerical order, and an undirected graph is, therefore, a nonlinear data structure. Let's consider another type of graph, the *directed graph*, which you can see in Figure 2-8.

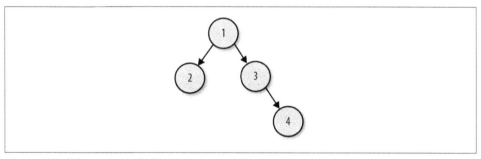

Figure 2-8. Directed graph diagram

The number of nodes is the same, but the edges look different. Instead of lines, they are arrows. There is a direction or flow between nodes in this graph. To represent it, we'd use the following:

```
vertices = {1, 2, 3, 4}
edges = ( {1, 2},
          {1, 3}
          {3, 4} )
```

All together, our graph equation would be as follows:

```
graph = ( {1, 2, 3, 4},
          ({1, 2}, {1, 3}, {3, 4})  )
```

Notice that the pairs are wrapped in parentheses rather than curly braces. The parentheses mean that these edge definitions are *ordered pairs*. Whenever the edges are ordered pairs, we have a directed graph or *digraph*. What would happen if we rearranged these ordered pairs? Would our diagram look the same, as was the case with the undirected graph?

```
graph = ( {1, 2, 3, 4},
          ( {4, 3}, {3, 1}, {1, 2} )  )
```

The resulting diagram would look quite different with node 4 now at the root, as illustrated in Figure 2-9.

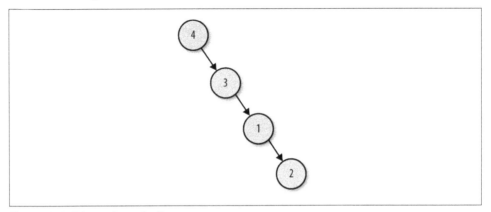

Figure 2-9. Directed graph diagram

To traverse the graph, you'd need to start travel at node 4 and visit each node of the graph by following the arrows. To help visualize traversal, it can be useful to picture physically traveling from one node to another. In fact, physical travel is how these graph theory concepts emerged.

History of Graph Theory

We can trace the study of graph theory back to the town of Königsberg, Prussia (*http://bit.ly/2AQhU47*) in 1735. Situated on the Pregel River, the town was a shipping hub that had two large islands connected by seven bridges to the four main landmasses, as Figure 2-10 shows.

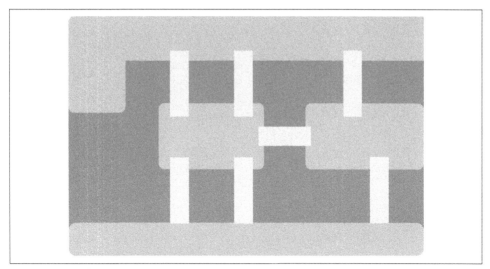

Figure 2-10. The Königsberg bridges

Königsberg was a gorgeous town, and the people of the town loved to spend their Sundays getting fresh air and walking the bridges. Over time, the townspeople became obsessed with trying to solve a puzzle: how could they cross over each of the seven bridges once without ever crossing back across the same bridge? They walked the town trying to visit each island and cross every bridge without repeating bridges but found themselves stuck. Hoping to get some help with the problem, they called upon Leonhard Euler. Euler was a prolific Swiss mathematician who published more than 500 books and papers during his lifetime.

Busy being a genius, Euler didn't care about what seemed like a trivial problem. But after giving it a bit more thought, Euler grew as interested as the residents of the town and tried feverishly to figure it out. Instead of writing down every possible path, Euler decided it would be simpler to look at the links (bridges) between the landmasses, as Figure 2-11 shows.

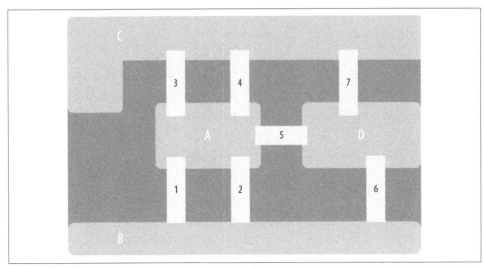

Figure 2-11. The Königsberg bridges numbered

He then simplified this, drawing the bridges and landmasses as what came to be known as a graph diagram. It looked like Figure 2-12:

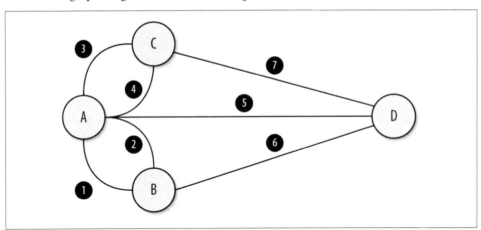

Figure 2-12. The Königsberg bridges as a diagram

In Figure 2-12, A and B are *adjacent* because they are connected by an edge. Using these edge connections, we can calculate the *degree* for each node. The degree of a node is equal to the number of edges that are attached to that node. If we look at the nodes in the Bridge Problem, we'll find that each of the degrees are odd.

- A: five edges to adjacent nodes (odd)
- B: three edges to adjacent nodes (odd)

- C: three edges to adjacent nodes (odd)
- D: three edges to adjacent nodes (odd)

Because each of the nodes had odd degrees, Euler found that crossing each bridge without recrossing was impossible. Long story short: if you take a bridge to get to an island, you must leave via a different bridge. The number of edges or bridges must be even if you don't want to recross a bridge.

Today, we call a graph in which each edge is visited once a *Eulerian path*. To qualify, the undirected graph will have two vertices with an odd degree or all vertices will have an even degree. Here, we have two vertices with an odd degree (1, 4), as seen in Figure 2-13.

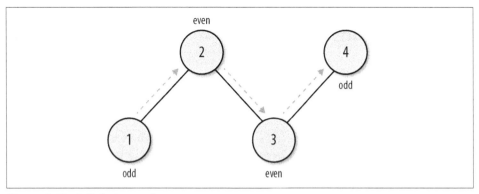

Figure 2-13. A Eulerian path

Another idea associated with Euler is a circuit or *Eulerian cycle*. In this case, the starting node is the same as the ending node. Each edge is visited only once, but the start and end node is repeated (Figure 2-14).

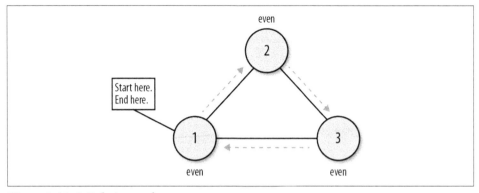

Figure 2-14. A Eulerian cycle

The Königsberg Bridge Problem became the first theorem of graph theory. In addition to being considered the originator of graph theory, Euler is known for creating the constant *e* and the *imaginary unit i*. Even the mathematical function syntax *f(x)*, a function *f* applied to the variable *x*, can be traced back to Leonhard Euler.[2]

The Königsberg Bridge Problem stated that a bridge could not be crossed more than once. There was never a rule that the journey must start or end at a specific node. This means that trying to solve the problem was an exercise in undirected graph traversal. What if you wanted to try to solve the bridge problem, but you had to start at a particular node?

If you live on island B, that's where you'd always have to start your traversal journey. In that case, you'd be dealing with a directed graph, more commonly called a tree.

Trees are Graphs

Let's consider another type of graph: a tree. A tree is a graph in which nodes are arranged hierarchically. You know you're looking at a tree if there is a root node. In other words, the root is where the tree starts, and then all of the other nodes are linked to the root as children.

Consider an organizational chart. This is a textbook tree. The CEO is at the top and all of the other employees are underneath the CEO. The CEO is the root of the tree and all of the other nodes are the root node's children, as Figure 2-15 shows.

---

2 More information about Euler and his work can be found at *http://www.storyofmathematics.com/18th_euler.html*.

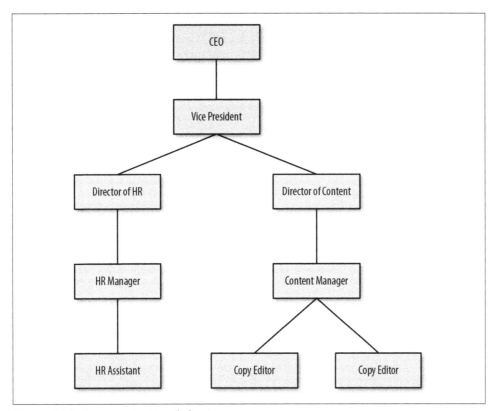

Figure 2-15. An organizational chart

Trees have many uses. You might use one to represent a family's genealogy. Trees can map decision-making algorithms. They help access information in databases quickly and efficiently. One day, you might even have to reverse a binary tree on a whiteboard for the five people standing between you and your new job where you'll never have to do that again.

We can determine whether a graph is a tree based on whether it has a root node or a starting node. From the root node, a tree is connected to child nodes by edges. When a node is connected to a child node, that node is called a parent. When a child has children, that node is referred to as a branch. When a node has no children, it is called a leaf.

Nodes contain data points. For that reason, it's important to understand where data is in the tree so that it can be quickly accessed. To find data quickly, we want to calculate the *depth* of individual nodes. The depth of a node simply refers to how far away the node is from the root of a tree. Let's consider the tree A -> B -> C -> D. To find the depth of node C, count the links between C and the root. There are exactly two links between C and the root (A), so the depth of node C is 2, and the depth of node D is 3.

The hierarchical structure of a tree means that trees often include other trees. A tree nested inside of a tree is called a subtree. An HTML page typically has several subtrees. The root of the tree is the <html> tag. Then, there are two subtrees with <head> at the root of the left subtree and <body> at the root of the right subtree. From there, <header>, <footer>, and <div> are all roots of different subtrees. With lots of nesting, there are a lot of subtrees, as Figure 2-16 depicts.

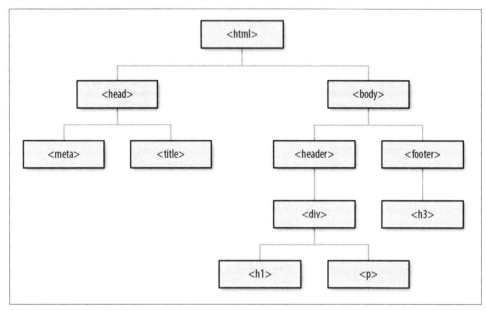

Figure 2-16. An HTML tree

Just as a tree is a specific type of graph, a *binary tree* is a specific type of tree. A binary tree means that each node has no more than two child nodes. When talking about binary trees, we're often referring to *binary search trees*.[3] A binary search tree is a binary tree that follows specific ordering rules. The ordering rules and tree structure help us to find the data that we need quickly. Figure 2-17 shows an example of a binary search tree.

---

3 See Vaidehi Joshi's blog post, "Leaf It Up to Binary Trees." (*http://bit.ly/2vQyKd5*)

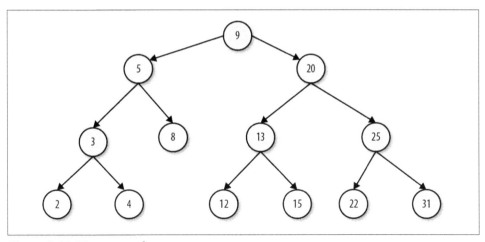

Figure 2-17. Binary search tree

It has a root node and follows the rule that each node should have no more than two child nodes. Suppose that we wanted to find node 15. Without a binary search tree, we'd need to visit every single node until we found node 15. Maybe we'd get lucky and go down the correct branch. Maybe we wouldn't be so lucky and would need to backtrack inefficiently around the tree.

With the binary search tree, we can locate node 15 skillfully by understanding the rules of left and right. If we begin traversal at the root (9), we'll say, "Is 15 greater than or less than 9?" If it's less than, we'll move to the left. If it's greater than, we'll move to the right. Fifteen is greater than 9, so we'll move right, and in doing so, we have excluded half of the nodes in the tree from our search. From here, we have node 20. Is 15 greater than or less than 20? It's less than, so we'll move to the left, eliminating half of the remaining nodes. Now at node 13, is 15 greater than or less than 13? It's greater than, so we'll head right. We've found it! By using left and right to eliminate options, we can find the data that we're interested in much more quickly.

Graphs in the Real World

You might encounter these graph theory concepts every day, depending on the work you do with GraphQL. Or, you might just be using GraphQL as an efficient way to load data into user interfaces. Regardless, all of these ideas are going on behind the scenes in GraphQL projects. As we've seen, graphs are particularly well suited to handle the needs of applications with a lot of data points.

Think of Facebook. With our graph theory vocabulary in place, we know that each person on Facebook is a node. When a person is connected with another person, there is a two-way connection via an edge. Facebook is an undirected graph. Whenever I connect to someone on Facebook, they are connected to me. My connection to my best friend, Sarah, is a two-way connection. We are friends with each other (as Figure 2-18 shows).

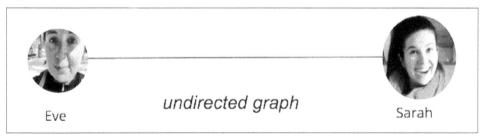

Figure 2-18. Facebook undirected graph

As an undirected graph, each node in the Facebook graph is part of a web of many interconnected relationships—a social network. You are connected to all of your friends. In the same graph, those friends are connected to all of their friends. Traversal can start and end at any node (Figure 2-19).

Figure 2-19. Facebook undirected web

Alternatively, there's Twitter. Unlike Facebook where everyone is paired in a two-way connection, Twitter is a directed graph because each connection is one way, as shown in Figure 2-20. If you follow Michelle Obama, she might not follow you back, even though she is always most welcome to do so (@eveporcello (*https://twitter.com/evepor cello*), @moontahoe (*https://twitter.com/moontahoe*)).

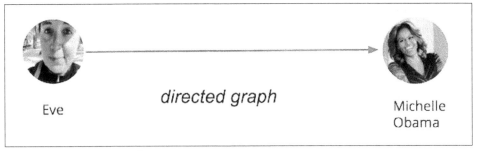

directed graph

Eve

Michelle
Obama

Figure 2-20. Twitter graph

If a person looks at all of her friendships, she becomes the root of a tree. She is connected to her friends. Then, her friends are connected to their friends in subtrees (Figure 2-21).

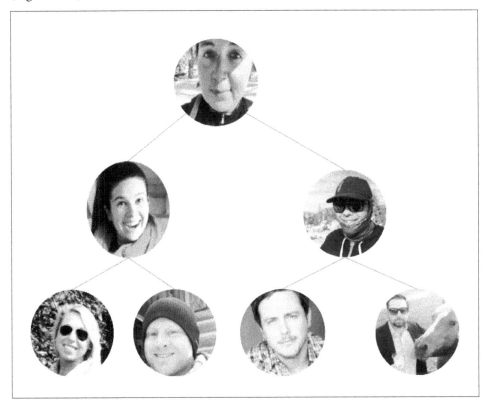

Figure 2-21. Friend tree

The same would be true for anyone else in the Facebook graph. As soon as you isolate a person and ask for their data, the request looks like a tree. The person is at the root, and all of the data that you want from that person is a child node. In this request, a person is connected to all of their friends by an edge:

- person
  — name
  — location
  — birthday
  — friends
      — friend name
      — friend location
      — friend birthday

This structure looks a lot like a GraphQL query:

```
{
    me {
        name
        location
        birthday
        friends {
            name
            location
            birthday
        }
    }
}
```

With GraphQL, we aim to simplify complex graphs of data by issuing queries for the data that we need. In the next chapter, we dig deeper into the mechanics of how a GraphQL query works and how a query is validated against a type system.

CHAPTER 3

The GraphQL Query Language

Forty-five years before GraphQL was open sourced, an IBM employee, Edgar M. Codd, released a fairly brief paper with a very long name. "A Relational Model of Data for Large Shared Databanks" (*http://bit.ly/2Ms7jxn*) didn't have a snappy title, but it contained some powerful ideas. It outlined a model for storing and manipulating data using tables. Soon after that, IBM began working on a relational database that could be queried using *Structured English Query Language*, or SEQUEL, which later became known only as *SQL*.

SQL, or Structured Query Language, is a domain-specific language used to access, manage, and manipulate data in a database. SQL introduced the idea of accessing multiple records with a single command. It also made it possible to access any record with any key, not just with an ID.

The commands that could be run with SQL were very streamlined: SELECT, INSERT, UPDATE, and DELETE. That's all you can do to data. With SQL, we can write a single query that can return connected data across multiple data tables in a database.

This idea—that data can only be read, created, updated, or deleted—did make its way to Representational State Transfer (REST), which requires us to use different HTTP methods depending upon these four basic data operations: GET, POST, PUT, and DELETE. However, the only way to specify what type of data you want to read or change with REST is via endpoint URLs, not an actual query language.

GraphQL takes the ideas that were originally developed to query databases and applies them to the internet. A single GraphQL query can return connected data. Like SQL, you can use GraphQL queries to change or remove data. After all, the QL in SQL and in GraphQL stand for the same thing: Query Language.

Even though they are both query languages, GraphQL and SQL are completely different. They are intended for completely different environments. You send SQL queries to a database. You send GraphQL queries to an API. SQL data is stored in data tables. GraphQL data can be stored anywhere: a database, multiple databases, file systems, REST APIs, WebSockets, even other GraphQL APIs. SQL is a query language for databases. GraphQL is a query language for the internet.

GraphQL and SQL also have entirely different syntax. Instead of SELECT, GraphQL uses `Query` to request data. This operation is at the heart of everything we do with GraphQL. Instead of INSERT, UPDATE, or DELETE, GraphQL wraps all of these data changes into one data type: the `Mutation`. Because GraphQL is built for the internet, it includes a `Subscription` type that can be used to listen for data changes over socket connections. SQL doesn't have anything like a subscription. SQL is like a grandparent that looks nothing like their grandchild, but we know they are related because they have the same last name.

GraphQL is standardized according to its spec. It doesn't matter what language you are using: a GraphQL query is a GraphQL query. The query syntax is a string that looks the same regardless of whether the project uses JavaScript, Java, Haskell, or anything else.

Queries are simply strings that are sent in the body of POST requests to a GraphQL endpoint. The following is a GraphQL query, a string written in the GraphQL query language:

```
{
  allLifts {
    name
  }
}
```

You would send this query to a GraphQL endpoint with *curl*:

```
curl 'http://snowtooth.herokuapp.com/'
  -H 'Content-Type: application/json'
  --data '{"query":"{ allLifts {name }}"}'
```

Assuming that the GraphQL schema supports a query of this shape, you will receive a JSON response directly in the terminal. That JSON response will contain either the data that you requested in a field named `data`, or the `errors` field if something went wrong. We make one request. We receive one response.

To modify data, we can send *mutations*. Mutations look a lot like queries, but their intention is to change something about the overall state of an application. The data required to perform a change can be sent directly with the mutation, as demonstrated here:

```
mutation {
  setLiftStatus(id: "panorama" status: OPEN) {
    name
    status
```

```
    }
}
```

The preceding mutation is written in the GraphQL query language and we can assume that it will change the status of a lift with an id of panorama to OPEN. Again, we can send this operation to a GraphQL server by using cURL:

```
curl 'http://snowtooth.herokuapp.com/'
  -H 'Content-Type: application/json'
  --data '{"query":"mutation {setLiftStatus(id: \"panorama\" status: OPEN) {name status}}"}'
```

There are fancier ways to map variables to a query or a mutation, but we cover those details later in the book. In this chapter, we focus on how to construct queries, mutations, and subscriptions using GraphQL.

GraphQL API Tools

The GraphQL community has produced several open source tools that you can use to interact with GraphQL APIs. These tools allow you to write queries in the GraphQL query language, send those queries to GraphQL endpoints, and inspect the JSON response. In this next section, we look at the two most popular tools for testing GraphQL queries against a GraphQL API: GraphiQL and GraphQL Playground.

GraphiQL

GraphiQL is the in-browser integrated development environment (IDE) that was created at Facebook to allow you to query and explore a GraphQL API. GraphiQL offers syntax highlighting, code completion, and error warnings, and it lets you run and view query results directly in the browser. Many public APIs provide a GraphiQL interface with which you can query live data.

The interface is fairly straightforward. There is a panel in which you write your query, a play button to run it, and a panel to display the response, as shown in Figure 3-1.

Figure 3-1. The GraphiQL interface

Our queries start off as text written in the GraphQL Query Language. We refer to this text as the *query document*. You place query text in the left panel. A GraphQL document can contain the definitions of one or more *operations*. An operation is a `Query`, `Mutation`, or `Subscription`. Figure 3-2 shows how you would add a `Query` operation to your document.

Figure 3-2. A GraphiQL query

Clicking the Play button runs the query. Then, in the right panel, you receive a response formatted as JSON (Figure 3-3).

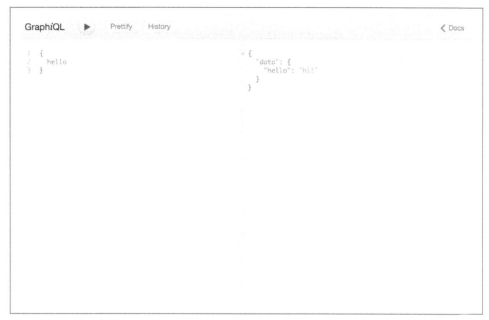

Figure 3-3. GraphiQL

In the upper-right corner, you can click to open the Docs window, which defines everything you need to know to interact with the current service. This documentation is automatically added to GraphiQL because it is read from the service's schema. The schema defines the data that is available on the service, and GraphiQL automatically builds documentation by running an introspection query against the schema. You can always view this documentation in the Documentation Explorer, as seen in Figure 3-4.

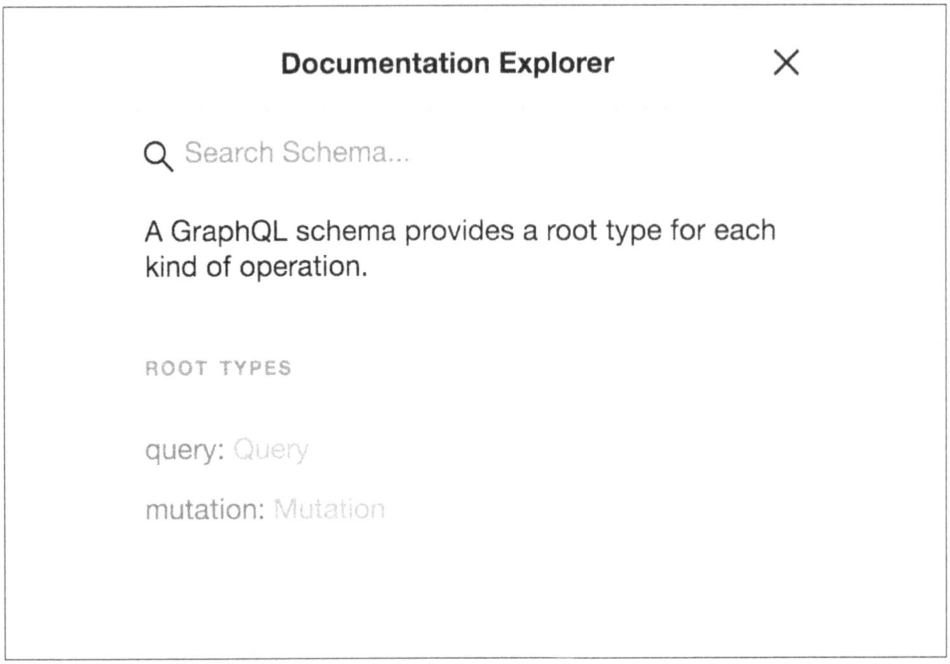

Documentation Explorer   ✕

🔍 Search Schema...

A GraphQL schema provides a root type for each
kind of operation.

ROOT TYPES

query: Query

mutation: Mutation

Figure 3-4. GraphiQL Documentation Explorer panel

More often than not, you will access GraphiQL via a URL that is hosted alongside the
GraphQL service itself. If you build your own GraphQL service, you can add a route
that renders the GraphQL interface so that your users can explore the data that you
make public to users. You also can download a standalone version of GraphiQL.

GraphQL Playground

Another tool for exploring GraphQL APIs is GraphQL Playground. Created by the
team at Prisma, *GraphQL Playground* mirrors the functionality of GraphiQL and adds
on a few interesting options. The easiest way to interact with a GraphQL Playground
is to check it out in the browser at *https://www.graphqlbin.com*. After you supply an
endpoint, you can interact with the data using the Playground.

The GraphQL Playground is very similar to GraphiQL, but it does come with several
extra features that you might find convenient. The most important feature is the ability to send custom HTTP headers along with your GraphQL request, as seen in
Figure 3-5 (We discuss this feature in greater detail when we cover authorization in
Chapter 5.)

Figure 3-5. GraphQL Playground

GraphQL Bin is also a fantastic collaboration tool because you can share links to your bins with others, as seen in Figure 3-6.

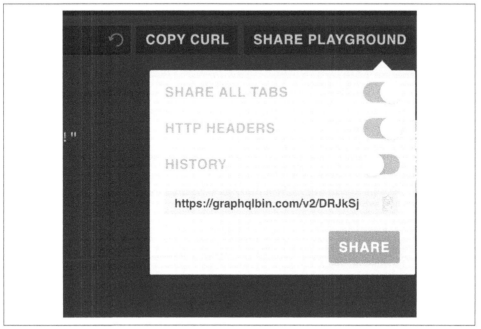

Figure 3-6. Sharing bins

GraphQL Playground has a desktop version that you can install locally using Homebrew:

```
brew cask install graphql-playground
```

Or, you can just download it from the website (*http://bit.ly/graphql-pg-releases*).

After you have this installed or have navigated to GraphQL Bin, you can begin sending queries. To get started quickly, you can paste an API endpoint in the playground. This could be a public API or your project running on a localhost port.

Public GraphQL APIs

One of the best ways to get started with GraphQL is to practice sending queries using a public API. Several companies and organizations provide a GraphiQL interface that you can use to query public data:

SWAPI (http://graphql.org/swapi-graphql) (the Star Wars API)
  This is a Facebook project that is a wrapper around the SWAPI REST API.

GitHub API (https://developer.github.com/v4/explorer/)
  One of the largest public GraphQL APIs, the GitHub GraphQL API allows you to send queries and mutations to view and change your live data on GitHub. You'll need to sign in with your GitHub account to interact with the data.

Yelp (https://www.yelp.com/developers/graphiql)
  Yelp maintains a GraphQL API that you can query using GraphiQL. You do need to create a Yelp developer account to interact with the data in the Yelp API.

Many additional examples (*https://github.com/APIs-guru/graphql-apis*) of public GraphQL APIs are available.

The GraphQL Query

Snowtooth Mountain is a fake ski resort. For the sake of the examples in this chapter, we will pretend it is a real mountain and that we work there. We are going to look at how the Snowtooth Mountain web team uses GraphQL to provide real-time, up-to-date information on chairlift status and trail status. The Snowtooth Ski Patrol can open and close chairlifts and trails directly from their phones. To follow along with the examples in this chapter, refer to Snowtooth's GraphQL Playground interface (*http://snowtooth.moonhighway.com*).

You can use the *query* operation to request data from an API. A query describes the data that you want to fetch from a GraphQL server. When you send a query, you ask for units of data by *field*. These fields map to the same field in the JSON data response you receive from your server. For example, if you send a query for `allLifts` and request the `name` and `status` fields, you should receive a JSON response that contains an array for `allLifts` and a string for each lift's `name` and each lift's `status`, as demonstrated here:

```
query {
  allLifts {
    name
    status
  }
}
```

Handling Errors

Successful queries return a JSON document that contains a "data" key. Unsuccessful queries return a JSON document that contains an "errors" key. The details of what went wrong is passed as JSON data under this key. A JSON response can contain both "data" and "errors."

You can add multiple queries to a query document, but you can run only one operation at a time. For example, you could place two query operations in a query document:

```
query lifts {
  allLifts {
    name
    status
  }
}

query trails {
  allTrails {
    name
    difficulty
  }
}
```

When you press the play button, the GraphQL Playground asks you to select one of these two operations. If you want to send one request for all of this data, you'll need to place it all within the same query:

```
query liftsAndTrails {
  liftCount(status: OPEN)
  allLifts {
    name
    status
  }
  allTrails {
    name
    difficulty
  }
}
```

Here is where the benefits of GraphQL begin to crystallize. We are able to receive all kinds of different datapoints in a single query. We are asking for the `liftCount` by status, which gives us the number of lifts that currently have that status. We are also asking for the `name` and `status` of every lift. Finally, we ask for the `name` and `status` of every trail in the same query.

A `Query` is a GraphQL type. We call it a *root type* because it's a type that maps to an operation, and operations represent the roots of our query document. The fields that are available to query in a GraphQL API have been defined in that API's schema. The documentation will tell us what fields are available to select on the `Query` type.

This documentation tells us that we are able to select the fields `liftCount`, `allLifts`, and `allTrails` when we query this API. It also defines more fields that are available to select, but the whole point of a query is that we get to choose which fields we need and which fields to omit.

When we write queries, we are selecting the fields that we need by encapsulating them in curly brackets. These blocks are referred to as *selection sets*. The fields that we define in a selection set are directly related to GraphQL types. The `liftCount`, `all Lifts`, and `allTrails` fields are defined in the `Query` type.

You can nest selection sets within one another. Because the `allLifts` field returns a list of `Lift` types, we need to use the curly brackets to create a new selection set on this type. There is all sorts of data that we can request about a lift, but in this example we want to select only the lift's `name` and `status`. Similarly, the `allTrails` query will return `Trail` types.

The JSON response contains all of the data that we requested in the query. This data is formatted as JSON and is delivered in the same shape as our query. Each JSON field is issued the same name as the field in our selection set. We can change the field names in the response object within the query by specifying an alias, as shown here:

```
query liftsAndTrails {
  open: liftCount(status: OPEN)
  chairlifts: allLifts {
    liftName: name
    status
  }
  skiSlopes: allTrails {
    name
    difficulty
  }
}
```

Following is the response:

```
{
  "data": {
    "open": 5,
```

```
    "chairlifts": [
      {
        "liftName": "Astra Express",
        "status": "open"
      }
    ],
    "skiSlopes": [
      {
        "name": "Ditch of Doom",
        "difficulty": "intermediate"
      }
    ]
  }
}
```

Now we get the data back in the same shape, but we have renamed several fields in our response. A way to filter the results of a GraphQL query is to pass in *query arguments*. Arguments are a key–value pair (or pairs) associated with a query field. If we want only the names of the closed chairlifts, we can send an argument that will filter our response:

```
query closedLifts {
    allLifts(status: "CLOSED" sortBy: "name") {
        name
        status
    }
}
```

You also can use arguments to select data. For instance, suppose that we want to query the status of an individual chairlift. We can select that chairlift by its unique identifier:

```
query jazzCatStatus {
    Lift(id: "jazz-cat") {
        name
        status
        night
        elevationGain
    }
}
```

Here we see the response contains the `name`, `status`, `night`, and `elevationGain` for the "Jazz Cat" chairlift.

Edges and Connections

In the GraphQL query language, fields can be either *scalar types* or *object types*. Scalar types are similar to primitives in other languages. They are the leaves of our selection sets. Out of the box, GraphQL comes with five built-in scalar types: integers (`Int`), floats (`Float`), strings (`String`), Booleans (`Boolean`), and unique identifiers (`ID`).

Both integers and floats return JSON numbers, and String and ID return JSON strings. Booleans just return Booleans. Even though ID and String will return the same type of JSON data, GraphQL still makes sure that IDs return unique strings.

GraphQL object types are groups of one or more fields that you define in your schema. They define the shape of the JSON object that should be returned. JSON can endlessly nest objects under fields, and so can GraphQL. We can connect objects together by querying one object for details about related objects.

For example, suppose that we want to receive a list of trails that we can access from a particular lift:

```
query trailsAccessedByJazzCat {
    Lift(id:"jazz-cat") {
        capacity
        trailAccess {
            name
            difficulty
        }
    }
}
```

In the preceding query, we are asking for some data about the "Jazz Cat" chairlift. Our selection set includes a request for the capacity field. Capacity is a scalar type; it returns an integer that represents the number of people that can ride on one chair. The trailAccess field is of type Trail (an object type). In this example, trailAccess returns a filtered list of trails that are accessible from Jazz Cat. Because trailAccess is a field within the Lift type, the API can use details about the parent object, the Jazz Cat Lift, to filter the list of returned trails.

This example operation queries a *one-to-many connection* between two types of data, lifts and trails. One lift is connected to many related trails. If we start our graph traversal from the Lift node, we can get to one or more Trail nodes that are connected to that lift via an edge that we have named trailAccess. For our graph to be considered undirected, we would need to traverse back to the Lift node from the Trail node, and we can:

```
query liftToAccessTrail {
    Trail(id:"dance-fight") {
        groomed
        accessedByLifts {
            name
            capacity
        }
    }
}
```

In the liftToAccessTrail query, we are selecting a Trail called "Dance Fight." The groomed field returns a Boolean scalar type that lets us know whether Dance Fight is groomed. The `accessedByLifts` field returns lifts that deliver skiers to the Dance Fight trail.

Fragments

A GraphQL query document can contain definitions for operations and *fragments*. Fragments are selection sets that can be reused in multiple operations. Take a look at the following query:

```
query {
    Lift(id: "jazz-cat") {
      name
      status
      capacity
      night
      elevationGain
      trailAccess {
        name
        difficulty
      }
    }
    Trail(id: "river-run") {
      name
      difficulty
      accessedByLifts {
        name
        status
        capacity
        night
        elevationGain
      }
    }
}
```

This query requests information about the Jazz Cat lift and the "River Run" trail. The `Lift` includes `name`, `status`, `capacity`, `night`, and `elevationGain` in its selection set. The information that we want to obtain about the River Run trail includes a subselection on the `Lift` type for the same fields. We could create a fragment that can help us reduce redundancy in our query:

```
fragment liftInfo on Lift {
  name
  status
  capacity
  night
  elevationGain
}
```

You create fragments by using the `fragment` identifier. Fragments are selection sets on specific types, so you must include the type that is associated with each fragment in its definition. The fragment in this example is named `liftInfo`, and it is a selection set on the `Lift` type.

When we want to add the `liftInfo` fragment fields to another selection set, we can do so by using three dots with the fragment name:

```
query {
    Lift(id: "jazz-cat") {
        ...liftInfo
        trailAccess {
          name
          difficulty
        }
    }
    Trail(id: "river-run") {
      name
      difficulty
      accessedByLifts {
        ...liftInfo
      }
    }
}
```

The syntax is similar to the JavaScript `spread` operator, which is used for a similar purpose—to assign the keys and values of one object to another. These three dots instruct GraphQL to assign the fields from the fragment to the current selection set. In this example, we are able to select the `name`, `status`, `capacity`, `night`, and `eleva tionGain` in two different places within our query using one fragment.

We would not be able to add the `liftInfo` fragment to the `Trail` selection set because it defines only fields on the `Lift` type. We can add another fragment for trails:

```
query {
    Lift(id: "jazz-cat") {
        ...liftInfo
        trailAccess {
          ...trailInfo
        }
    }
    Trail(id: "river-run") {
        ...trailInfo
        groomed
        trees
        night
    }
}

fragment trailInfo on Trail {
  name
  difficulty
```

```
    accessedByLifts {
      ...liftInfo
    }
  }

  fragment liftInfo on Lift {
    name
    status
    capacity
    night
    elevationGain
  }
```

In this example, we have created a fragment called `trailInfo` and used it in two places within our query. We're also using the `liftInfo` fragment in the `trailInfo` fragment to select details about the connected lifts. You can create as many fragments as you want and use them interchangeably. In the selection set used by the River Run Trail query, we are combining our fragment with additional details that we want to select about the River Run trail. You can use fragments in combination with other fields in a selection set. You also can combine multiple fragments on the same type in a single selection set:

```
query {
  allTrails {
    ...trailStatus
    ...trailDetails
  }
}

fragment trailStatus on Trail {
  name
  status
}

fragment trailDetails on Trail {
  groomed
  trees
  night
}
```

One nice thing about fragments is that you can modify the selection sets used in many different queries simply by modifying one fragment:

```
fragment liftInfo on Lift {
  name
  status
}
```

This change to the selection set in the `liftInfo` fragment causes every query that is using this fragment to select less data.

Union types

We've already looked at how to return lists of objects, but in each case so far, we've returned lists of a single type. If you wanted a list to return more than one type, you could create a *union type*, which creates an association between two different object types.

Suppose that we're building a scheduling app for college students with which they can add Workout and Study Group events to an agenda. You can check out this running sample at *https://rm2rx3opqm.sse.codesandbox.io*.

If you look at the documentation in GraphQL Playground, you will see that an Agen daItem is a union type, which means that it can return multiple types. Specifically, the AgendaItem can return a Workout or StudyGroup, which are things that might be part of a college student's schedule.

When writing a query for a student's agenda, you can use fragments to define which fields to select when the AgendaItem is a Workout, and which fields to select when the AgendaItem is a StudyGroup:

```
query schedule {
    agenda {
    ...on Workout {
      name
      reps
    }
    ...on StudyGroup {
      name
      subject
      students
    }
  }
}
```

Here's the response:

```
{
  "data": {
    "agenda": [
      {
        "name": "Comp Sci",
        "subject": "Computer Science",
        "students": 12
      },
      {
        "name": "Cardio",
        "reps": 100
      },
      {
        "name": "Poets",
        "subject": "English 101",
```

```
          "students": 3
        },
        {
          "name": "Math Whiz",
          "subject": "Mathematics",
          "students": 12
        },
        {
          "name": "Upper Body",
          "reps": 10
        },
        {
          "name": "Lower Body",
          "reps": 20
        }
      ]
    }
  }
```

Here, we are using *inline fragments*. Inline fragments do not have names. They assign selection sets to specific types directly within the query. We use them to define which fields to select when a union returns different types of objects. For each Workout, this query asks for the names and the reps in the returned Workout object. For each study group, we ask for the name, subject, and students in the returned StudyGroup object. The returned agenda will consist of a single array that contains different types of objects.

You can also use named fragments to query a union type:

```
query today {
    agenda {
    ...workout
    ...study
  }
}

fragment workout on Workout {
  name
  reps
}

fragment study on StudyGroup {
  name
  subject
  students
}
```

Interfaces

Interfaces are another option when dealing with multiple object types that could be returned by a single field. An interface is an abstract type that establishes a list of fields that should be implemented in similar object types. When another type implements the interface, it includes all of the fields from the interface and usually some of its own fields. If you'd like to follow along with this sample, you can find it on GraphQL Bin (*https://71x8n304r1.sse.codesandbox.io*).

When you look at the agenda field in the documentation, you can see that it returns the ScheduleItem interface. This interface defines the fields: name, start time, and end time. Any object type that implements the ScheduleItem interface needs to implement these fields.

The documentation also informs us that the StudyGroup and Workout types implement this interface. This means that we can safely assume that both of these types have fields for name, start, and end:

```
query schedule {
  agenda {
    name
    start
    end
  }
}
```

The schedule query doesn't seem to care that the agenda field returns multiple types. It needs only the name, start, and end times for the item in order to create the schedule of when and where this student should be.

When querying an interface, we can also use fragments to select additional fields when a specific object type is returned:

```
query schedule {
  agenda {
    name
    start
    end
    ...on Workout {
      reps
    }
  }
}
```

The schedule query has been modified to additionally request the reps when the ScheduleItem is a Workout.

Mutations

So far, we've talked a lot about reading data. Queries describe all of the *reads* that happen in GraphQL. To write new data, we use *mutations*. Mutations are defined like queries. They have names. They can have selection sets that return object types or scalars. The difference is that mutations perform some sort of a data change that affects the state of your backend data.

For example, a dangerous mutation to implement would look like this:

```
mutation burnItDown {
  deleteAllData
}
```

The `Mutation` is a root object type. The API's schema defines the fields that are available on this type. The API in the preceding example has the power to wipe out all data to the client by implementing a field called `deleteAllData` that returns a scalar type: `true` if all of the data was successfully deleted and it's time to start looking for a new job, or `false` if something went wrong and it's time to start looking for a new job. Whether the data is actually deleted is handled by the implementation of the API, which we discuss further in Chapter 5.

Let's consider another mutation. But instead of destroying something, let's create something:

```
mutation createSong {
  addSong(title:"No Scrubs", numberOne: true, performerName:"TLC") {
    id
    title
    numberOne
  }
}
```

We can use this example to create new songs. The `title`, `numberOne` status, and `performerName` are sent to this mutation as arguments, and we can assume that the mutation adds this new song to a database. If the mutation field returns an object, you will need to add a selection set after the mutation. In this case, after it's completed, the mutation will return the `Song` type that contains details about the song that was just created. We can select the `id`, `title`, and `numberOne` status of the new song after the mutation:

```
{
  "data": {
    "addSong": {
      "id": "5aca534f4bb1de07cb6d73ae",
      "title": "No Scrubs",
      "numberOne": true
    }
  }
}
```

The preceding is an example of what the response to this mutation might look like. If something went wrong, the mutation would return the error in the JSON response instead of our newly created `Song` object.

We also can use mutations to change existing data. Suppose that we want to change the status of a Snowtooth chairlift. We could use a mutation to do that:

```
mutation closeLift {
    setLiftStatus(id: "jazz-cat" status: CLOSED) {
      name
      status
  }
}
```

We can use this mutation to change the status of the Jazz Cat lift from open to closed. After the mutation, we can then select fields on the `Lift` that was recently changed in our selection set. In this case, we get the `name` of the lift that was changed and the new `status`.

Using Query Variables

So far, we have changed data by sending new string values as mutation arguments. As an alternative, you could use input *variables*. Variables replace the static value in the query so that we can pass dynamic values, instead. Let's consider our `addSong` mutation. Instead of dealing with strings, let's use variable names, which in GraphQL are always preceded by a $ character:

```
mutation createSong($title:String! $numberOne:Int $by:String!) {
    addSong(title:$title, numberOne:$numberOne, performerName:$by) {
      id
      title
      numberOne
  }
}
```

The static value is replaced by a `$variable`. Then, we state that the `$variable` can be accepted by the mutation. From there, we map each of the `$variable` names with the argument name. In GraphiQL or the Playground, there is a window for Query Variables. This is where we send the input data as a JSON object. Be sure to use the correct variable name as the JSON key:

```
{
  "title": "No Scrubs",
  "numberOne": true,
  "by": "TLC"
}
```

Variables are very useful when sending argument data. Not only will this keep our mutations more organized in a test, but allowing dynamic inputs will be hugely helpful later when connecting a client interface.

Subscriptions

The third type of operation available with GraphQL is the subscription. There are times when a client might want to have real-time updates pushed from the server. A subscription allows us to listen to the GraphQL API for real-time data changes.

Subscriptions in GraphQL came from a real-life use case at Facebook. The team wanted a way to show real-time information about the number of likes (Live Likes) that a post was getting without refreshing the page. Live Likes are a real-time use case that is powered by subscriptions. Every client is subscribed to the like event and sees likes being updated in real time.

Just like the mutation and the query, a subscription is a root type. Data changes clients can listen to are defined in an API schema as fields under the subscription type. Writing the GraphQL query to listen for a subscription is also similar to how we would define other operations.

For example, with Snowtooth (*http://snowtooth.moonhighway.com*), we can listen for the status change of any lift with a subscription:

```
subscription {
  liftStatusChange {
    name
    capacity
    status
  }
}
```

When we run this subscription, we listen for lift status changes over a WebSocket. Notice that clicking the play button in the GraphQL Playground doesn't immediately return data. When the subscription is sent to the server, the subscription is listening for any changes to the data.

To see data pushed to the subscription, we need to make a change. We need to open a new window or tab to send that change via a mutation. After a subscription operation is running in a GraphQL Playground tab, we cannot run anymore operations using the same window or tab. If you are using GraphiQL to write subscriptions, simply open a second browser window to the GraphiQL interface. If you are using the GraphQL Playground, you can open a new tab to add the mutation.

From the new window or tab, let's send a lift status change mutation:

```
mutation closeLift {
  setLiftStatus(id: "astra-express" status: HOLD) {
    name
    status
  }
}
```

When we run this mutation, the status of "Astra Express" will change and the name, capacity, and status of the Astra Express lift are pushed to our subscription. Astra Express is the last lift that has changed and the new status is pushed to the subscription.

Let's change the status of a second lift. Try to set the status of the "Whirlybird" lift to closed. Notice that this new information has been passed to our subscription. The GraphQL Playground allows you to see both sets of response data along with the time that the data was pushed to the subscription.

Unlike queries and mutations, subscriptions remain open. New data will be pushed to this subscription every time there is a status change on a chairlift. To stop listening for status changes, you need to unsubscribe from your subscription. To do this with the GraphQL Playground, simply press the stop button. Unfortunately, the only way to unsubscribe from a subscription with GraphiQL is to close the browser tab on which the subscription is running.

Introspection

One of the most powerful features of GraphQL is *introspection*. Introspection is the ability to query details about the current API's schema. Introspection is how those nifty GraphQL documents are added to the GraphiQL Playground interface.

You can send queries to every GraphQL API that return data about a given API's schema. For example, if we want to know what GraphQL types are available to us in Snowtooth, we can view that information by running a __schema query, as demonstrated here:

```
query {
  __schema {
    types {
      name
      description
    }
  }
}
```

When we run this query, we see every type available on the API, including root types, custom types, and even scalar types. If we want to see the details of a particular type, we can run the __type query and send the name of the type that we want to query as an argument:

```
query liftDetails {
  __type(name:"Lift") {
    name
    fields {
      name
      description
```

```
      type {
        name
      }
    }
  }
}
```

This introspection query shows us all of the fields that are available to query on the
Lift type. When getting to know a new GraphQL API, it is a good idea to find out
what fields are available on the root types:

```
query roots {
  __schema {
    queryType {
      ...typeFields
    }
    mutationType {
      ...typeFields
    }
    subscriptionType {
      ...typeFields
    }
  }
}

fragment typeFields on __Type {
  name
  fields {
    name
  }
}
```

An introspection query follows the rules of the GraphQL query language. The redundancy of the preceding query has been reduced by using a fragment. We are querying
the name of the type and the available fields of each root type. Introspection gives the
client the ability to find out how the current API schema works.

Abstract Syntax Trees

The query document is a string. When we send a query to a GraphQL API, that string
is parsed into an *abstract syntax tree* and validated before the operation is run. An
abstract syntax tree, or AST, is a hierarchical object that represents our query. The
AST is an object that contains nested fields that represent the details of a GraphQL
query.

The first step in this process is to parse the string into a bunch of smaller pieces. This
includes parsing the keywords, arguments, and even brackets and colons into a set of
individual tokens. This process is called *lexing*, or *lexical analysis*. Next, the lexed

query is parsed into an AST. A query is much easier to dynamically modify and validate as an AST.

For example, your queries start off as a GraphQL *document*. A document contains at least one *definition*, but it can also contain a list of definitions. Definitions are only one of two types: `OperationDefinition` or `FragmentDefinition`. The following is an example of a document that contains three definitions: two operations, and one fragment:

```
query jazzCatStatus {
    Lift(id: "jazz-cat") {
      name
      night
      elevationGain
      trailAccess {
        name
        difficulty
      }
    }
}

mutation closeLift($lift: ID!) {
  setLiftStatus(id: $lift, status: CLOSED ) {
    ...liftStatus
  }
}

fragment liftStatus on Lift {
  name
  status
}
```

An `OperationDefinition` can contain only one of three operation types: `mutation`, `query`, or `subscription`. Each operation definition contains the `OperationType` and the `SelectionSet`.

The curly brackets that come after each operation contain the operation's `Selection Set`. These are the actual fields that we are querying along with their arguments. For example, the `Lift` field is the `SelectionSet` for the `jazzCatStatus` query and the `setLiftStatus` field represents the selection set for the `closeLift` mutation.

Selection sets are nested within one another. The `jazzCatStatus` query has three nested selection sets. The first `SelectionSet` contains the `Lift` field. Nested within is a `SelectionSet` that contains the field: `name`, `night`, `elevationGain`, and `trailAccess`. Nested under the `trailAccess` field is another `SelectionSet` that contains the `name` and `difficulty` fields for each trail.

GraphQL can traverse this AST and validate its details against the GraphQL language and the current schema. If the query language syntax is correct and the schema con-

---

tains the fields and types that we are requesting, the operation is executed. If not, a specific error is returned, instead.

Additionally, this AST object is easier to modify than a string. If we wanted to append the number of open lifts to the `jazzCatStatus` query, we could do so by directly modifying the AST. All we need to do is add an additional `SelectionSet` to the operation. ASTs are an essential part of GraphQL. Every operation is parsed into an AST so that it can be validated and eventually executed.

In this chapter, you learned about the GraphQL query language. We can now use this language to interact with a GraphQL service. But, none of this would be possible without a specific definition of what operations and fields are available on a particular GraphQL service. This specific definition is called the *GraphQL schema*, and we take a closer look at how to create schemas in the next chapter.

CHAPTER 4

Designing a Schema

GraphQL is going to change your design process. Instead of looking at your APIs as a collection of REST endpoints, you are going to begin looking at your APIs as collections of types. Before breaking ground on your new API, you need to think about, talk about, and formally define the data types that your API will expose. This collection of types is called a *schema*.

Schema First is a design methodology that will get all of your teams on the same page about the data types that make up your application. The backend team will have a clear understanding about the data that it needs to store and deliver. The frontend team will have the definitions that it needs to begin building user interfaces. Everyone will have a clear vocabulary that they can use to communicate about the system they are building. In short, everyone can get to work.

To facilitate defining types, GraphQL comes with a language that we can use to define our schemas, called the *Schema Definition Language*, or SDL. Just like the GraphQL Query Language, the GraphQL SDL is the same no matter what language or framework you use to construct your applications. GraphQL schema documents are text documents that define the types available in an application, and they are later used by both clients and servers to validate GraphQL requests.

In this chapter, we take a look at the GraphQL SDL and build a schema for a photo sharing application.

Defining Types

The best way to learn about GraphQL types and schemas is to build one. The photo sharing application will let users log in with their GitHub accounts to post photos and tag users in those photos. Managing users and posts represents functionality that is core to just about every type of internet application.

The PhotoShare application will have two main types: `User` and `Photo`. Let's get started designing the schema for the entire application.

Types

The core unit of any GraphQL Schema is the type. In GraphQL, a *type* represents a custom object and these objects describe your application's core features. For example, a social media application consists of `Users` and `Posts`. A blog would consist of `Categories` and `Articles`. The types represent your application's data.

If you were to build Twitter from scratch, a `Post` would contain the text that the user wishes to broadcast. (In this case, a `Tweet` might be a better name for that type.) If you were building Snapchat, a `Post` would contain an image and would more appropriately be named a `Snap`. When defining a schema, you will define a common language that your team will use when talking about your domain objects.

A type has *fields* that represent the data associated with each object. Each field returns a specific type of data. This could mean an integer or a string, but it also could mean a custom object type or list of types.

A schema is a collection of type definitions. You can write your schemas in a JavaScript file as a string or in any text file. These files usually carry the `.graphql` extension.

Let's define the first GraphQL object type in our schema file—the `Photo`:

```
type Photo {
    id: ID!
    name: String!
    url: String!
    description: String
}
```

Between the curly brackets, we've defined the `Photo`'s fields. The `Photo`'s `url` is a reference to the location of the image file. This description also contains some metadata about the `Photo`: a `name` and a `description`. Finally, each `Photo` will have an `ID`, a unique identifier that can be used as a key to access the photo.

Each field contains data of a specific type. We have defined only one custom type in our schema, the `Photo`, but GraphQL comes with some built-in types that we can use for our fields. These built-in types are called *scalar types*. The `description`, `name`, and `url` fields use the `String` scalar type. The data that is returned when we query these fields will be JSON strings. The exclamation point specifies that the field is *non-nullable*, which means that the `name` and `url` fields must return some data in each query. The `description` is *nullable*, which means that photo descriptions are optional. When queried, this field could return `null`.

The Photo's ID field specifies a unique identifier for each photo. In GraphQL, the ID scalar type is used when a unique identifier should be returned. The JSON value for this identifier will be a string, but this string will be validated as a unique value.

Scalar Types

GraphQL's built in scalar types (Int, Float, String, Boolean, ID) are very useful, but there might be times when you want to define your own custom scalar types. A scalar type is not an object type. It does not have fields. However, when implementing a GraphQL service, you can specify how custom scalar types should be validated; for example:

```
scalar DateTime

type Photo {
    id: ID!
    name: String!
    url: String!
    description: String
    created: DateTime!
}
```

Here, we have created a custom scalar type: DateTime. Now we can find out when each photo was created. Any field marked DateTime will return a JSON string, but we can use the custom scalar to make sure that string can be serialized, validated, and formatted as an official date and time.

You can declare custom scalars for any type that you need to validate.

> The graphql-custom-types npm package contains some commonly used custom scalar types that you can quickly add to your Node.js GraphQL service.

Enums

Enumeration types, or *enums*, are scalar types that allow a field to return a restrictive set of string values. When you want to make sure that a field returns one value from a limited set of values, you can use an enum type.

For example, let's create an enum type called PhotoCategory that defines the type of photo that is being posted from a set of five possible choices: SELFIE, PORTRAIT, ACTION, LANDSCAPE, or GRAPHIC:

```
enum PhotoCategory {
    SELFIE
    PORTRAIT
```

```
        ACTION
        LANDSCAPE
        GRAPHIC
    }
```

You can use enumeration types when defining fields. Let's add a `category` field to our Photo object type:

```
type Photo {
    id: ID!
    name: String!
    url: String!
    description: String
    created: DateTime!
    category: PhotoCategory!
}
```

Now that we have added `category`, we will make sure that it returns one of the five valid values when we implement the service.

 It does not matter whether your implementation has full support for enumeration types. You can implement GraphQL enumeration fields in any language.

Connections and Lists

When you create GraphQL schemas, you can define fields that return lists of any GraphQL type. Lists are created by surrounding a GraphQL type with square brackets. `[String]` defines a list of strings and `[PhotoCategory]` defines a list of photo categories. As Chapter 3 discusses, lists can also consist of multiple types if we incorporate `union` or `interface` types. We discuss these types of lists in greater detail toward the end of this chapter.

Sometimes, the exclamation point can be a little tricky when defining lists. When the exclamation point comes after the closing square bracket, it means that the field itself is non-nullable. When the exclamation point comes before the closing square bracket, it means that the values contained in the list are non-nullable. Wherever you see an exclamation point, the value is required and cannot return null. Table 4-1 defines these various situations.

Table 4-1. Nullability rules with lists

list declaration	definition
`[Int]`	A list of nullable integer values
`[Int!]`	A list of non-nullable integer values

list declaration	definition
[Int]!	A non-nullable list of nullable integer values
[Int!]!	A non-nullable list of non-nullable integer values

Most list definitions are non-nullable lists of non-nullable values. This is because we typically do not want values within our list to be null. We should filter out any null values ahead of time. If our list doesn't contain any values, we can simply return an empty JSON array; for example, [ ]. An empty array is technically not null: it is just an array that doesn't contain any values.

The ability to connect data and query multiple types of related data is a very important feature. When we create lists of our custom object types, we are using this powerful feature and connecting objects to one another.

In this section, we cover how to use a list to connect object types.

One-to-One Connections

When we create fields based on custom object types, we are connecting two objects. In graph theory, a connection or link between two objects is called an *edge*. The first type of connection is a one-to-one connection in which we connect a single object type to another single object type.

Photos are posted by users, so every photo in our system should contain an edge connecting the photo to the user who posted it. Figure 4-1 shows a one-way connection between two types: Photo and User. The edge that connects the two nodes is called postedBy.

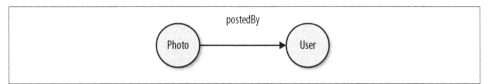

Figure 4-1. One-to-one connection

Let's see how we would define this in the schema:

```
type User {
    githubLogin: ID!
    name: String
    avatar: String
}

type Photo {
    id: ID!
    name: String!
    url: String!
```

```
        description: String
        created: DateTime!
        category: PhotoCategory!
        postedBy: User!
    }
```

First, we've added a new type to our schema, the User. The users of the PhotoShare application are going to sign in via GitHub. When the user signs in, we obtain their githubLogin and use it as the unique identifier for their user record. Optionally, if they added their name or photo to GitHub, we will save that information under the fields name and avatar.

Next, we added the connection by adding a postedBy field to the photo object. Each photo must be posted by a user, so this field is set to the User! type; the exclamation point is added to make this field non-nullable.

One-to-Many Connections

It is a good idea to keep GraphQL services undirected when possible. This provides our clients with the ultimate flexibility to create queries because they can start traversing the graph from any node. All we need to do to follow this practice is provide a path back from User types to Photo types. This means that when we query a User, we should get to see all of the photos that particular user posted:

```
type User {
    githubLogin: ID!
    name: String
    avatar: String
    postedPhotos: [Photo!]!
}
```

By adding the postedPhotos field to the User type, we have provided a path back to the Photo from the user. The postedPhotos field will return a list of Photo types, those photos posted by the parent user. Because one user can post many photos, we've created a one-to-many connection. One-to-many connections, as shown in Figure 4-2, are common connections that are created when a parent object contains a field that lists other objects.

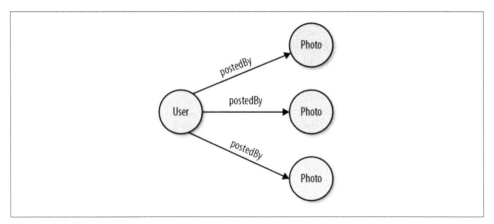

Figure 4-2. One-to-many connection

A common place to add one-to-many connections is in our root types. To make our photos or users available in a query, we need to define the fields of our Query root type. Let's take a look at how we can add our new custom types to the Query root type:

```
type Query {
    totalPhotos: Int!
    allPhotos: [Photo!]!
    totalUsers: Int!
    allUsers: [User!]!
}

schema {
    query: Query
}
```

Adding the Query type defines the queries that are available in our API. In this example, we've added two queries for each type: one to deliver the total number of records available on each type, and another to deliver the full list of those records. Additionally, we've added the Query type to the schema as a file. This makes our queries available in our GraphQL API.

Now our photos and users can be queried with the following query string:

```
query {
    totalPhotos
    allPhotos {
        name
        url
    }
}
```

Many-to-Many Connections

Sometimes we want to connect lists of nodes to other lists of nodes. Our PhotoShare application will allow users to identify other users in each photo that they post. This process is called *tagging*. A photo can consist of many users, and a user can be tagged in many photos, as Figure 4-3 shows.

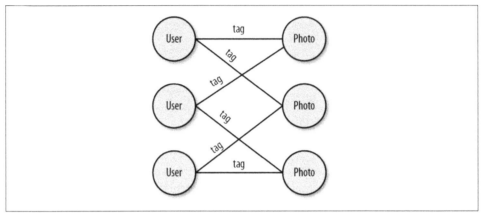

Figure 4-3. Many-to-many connection

To create this type of connection, we need to add list fields to both the User and the Photo types.

```
type User {
    ...
    inPhotos: [Photo!]!
}

type Photo {
    ...
    taggedUsers: [User!]!
}
```

As you can see, a *many-to-many* connection consists of two *one-to-many* connections. In this case, a Photo can have many tagged users, and a User can be tagged in many photos.

Through types

Sometimes, when creating many-to-many relationships, you might want to store some information about the relationship itself. Because there is no real need for a through type in our photo sharing app, we are going to use a different example to define a through type, a friendship between users.

We can connect many users to many users by defining a field under a User that contains a list of other users:

```
type User {
    friends: [User!]!
}
```

Here, we've defined a list of friends for each user. Consider a case in which we wanted to save some information about the friendship itself, like how long users have known one another or where they met.

In this situation, we need to define the edge as a custom object type. We call this object a *through type* because it is a node that is designed to connect two nodes. Let's define a through type called Friendship that we can use to connect two friends but also deliver data on how the friends are connected:

```
type User {
    friends: [Friendship!]!
}
type Friendship {
    friend_a: User!
    friend_b: User!
    howLong: Int!
    whereWeMet: Location
}
```

Instead of defining the friends field directly on a list of other User types, we've created a Friendship to connect the friends. The Friendship type defines the two connected friends: friend_a and friend_b. It also defines some detail fields about how the friends are connected: howLong and whereWeMet. The howLong field is an Int that will define the length of the friendship, and the whereWeMet field links to a custom type called Location.

We can improve upon the design of the Friendship type by allowing for a group of friends to be a part of the friendship. For example, maybe you met your best friends at the same time in first grade. We can allow for two or more friends to be a part of the friendship by adding a single field called friends:

```
type Friendship {
    friends: [User!]!
    how_long: Int!
    where_we_met: Location
}
```

We've only included one field for all of the friends in a Friendship. Now this type can reflect two or more friends.

Lists of Different Types

In GraphQL, our lists do not always need to return the same type. In Chapter 3, we introduced union types and interfaces, and we learned how to write queries for these types using fragments. Let's take a look at how we can add these types to our schema.

Here, we will use a schedule as an example. You might have a schedule made up of different events, each requiring different data fields. For instance, the details about a study group meeting or a workout might be completely different, but you should be able to add both to a schedule. You can think of a daily schedule as a list of different types of activities.

There are two ways in which we can handle defining a schema for a schedule in GraphQL: unions and interfaces.

Union types

In GraphQL, a *union type* is a type that we can use to return one of several different types. Recall from Chapter 3 how we wrote a query called schedule that queried an agenda and returned different data when the agenda item was a workout than when it was a study group. Let's take a look at it again here:

```
query schedule {
    agenda {
        ...on Workout {
            name
            reps
        }
        ...on StudyGroup {
            name
            subject
            students
        }
    }
}
```

In the student's daily agenda, we could handle this by creating a union type called AgendaItem:

```
union AgendaItem = StudyGroup | Workout

type StudyGroup {
    name: String!
    subject: String
    students: [User!]!
}

type Workout {
    name: String!
```

```
        reps: Int!
    }

    type Query {
        agenda: [AgendaItem!]!
    }
```

AgendaItem combines study groups and workouts under a single type. When we add the agenda field to our Query, we are defining it as a list of either workouts or study groups.

It is possible to join as many types as we want under a single union. Simply separate each type with a pipe:

```
    union = StudyGroup | Workout | Class | Meal | Meeting | FreeTime
```

Interfaces

Another way of handling fields that could contain multiple types is to use an interface. *Interfaces* are abstract types that can be implemented by object types. An interface defines all of the fields that must be included in any object that implements it. Interfaces are a great way to organize code within your schema. This ensures that certain types always include specific fields that are queryable no matter what type is returned.

In Chapter 3, we wrote a query for an agenda that used an interface to return fields on different items in a schedule. Let's review that here:

```
    query schedule {
      agenda {
        name
        start
        end
        ...on Workout {
          reps
        }
      }
    }
```

Here is what it might look like to query an agenda that implemented interfaces. For a type to interface with our schedule, it must contain specific fields that all agenda items will implement. These fields include name, start, and end times. It doesn't matter what type of schedule item you have, they all need these details in order to be listed on a schedule.

Here is how we would implement this solution in our GraphQL schema:

```
    scalar DataTime

    interface AgendaItem {
        name: String!
```

```
        start: DateTime!
        end: DateTime!
    }

    type StudyGroup implements AgendaItem {
        name: String!
        start: DateTime!
        end: DateTime!
        participants: [User!]!
        topic: String!
    }

    type Workout implements AgendaItem {
        name: String!
        start: DateTime!
        end: DateTime!
        reps: Int!
    }

    type Query {
        agenda: [AgendaItem!]!
    }
```

In this example, we create an interface called `AgendaItem`. This interface is an abstract type that other types can implement. When another type implements an interface, it must contain the fields defined by the interface. Both `StudyGroup` and `Workout` implement the `AgendaItem` interface, so they both need to use the `name`, `start`, and `end` fields. The query `agenda` returns a list of `AgendaItem` types. Any type that implements the `AgendaItem` interface can be returned in the `agenda` list.

Also notice that these types can implement other fields, as well. A `StudyGroup` has a `topic` and a list of `participants`, and a `Workout` still has `reps`. You can select these additional fields in a query by using fragments.

Both union types and interfaces are tools that you can use to create fields that contain different object types. It's up to you to decide when to use one or the other. In general, if the objects contain completely different fields, it is a good idea to use union types. They are very effective. If an object type must contain specific fields in order to interface with another type of object, you will need to use an interface rather than a union type.

Arguments

Arguments can be added to any field in GraphQL. They allow us to send data that can affect outcome of our GraphQL operations. In Chapter 3, we looked at user arguments within our queries and mutations. Now, let's take a look at how we would define arguments in our schema.

The Query type contains fields that will list allUsers or allPhotos, but what happens when you want to select only one User or one Photo? You would need to supply some information on the one user or photo that you would like to select. You can send that information along with my query as an argument:

```
type Query {
    ...
    User(githubLogin: ID!): User!
    Photo(id: ID!): Photo!
}
```

Just like a field, an argument must have a type. That type can be defined using any of the scalar types or object types that are available in our schema. To select a specific user, we need to send that user's unique githubLogin as an argument. The following query selects only MoonTahoe's name and avatar:

```
query {
    User(githubLogin: "MoonTahoe") {
        name
        avatar
    }
}
```

To select details about an individual photo, we need to supply that photo's ID:

```
query {
    Photo(id: "14TH5B6NS4KIG3H4S") {
        name
        description
        url
    }
}
```

In both cases, arguments were required to query details about one specific record. Because these arguments are required, they are defined as non-nullable fields. If we do not supply the id or githubLogin with these queries, the GraphQL parser will return an error.

Filtering Data

Arguments do not need to be non-nullable. We can add optional arguments using nullable fields. This means that we can supply arguments as optional parameters when we execute query operations. For example, we could filter the photo list that is returned by the allPhotos query by photo category:

```
type Query {
    ...
    allPhotos(category: PhotoCategory): [Photo!]!
}
```

We have added an optional `category` field to the `allPhotos` query. The category must match the values of the enumeration type `PhotoCategory`. If a value is not sent with the query, we can assume that this field will return every photo. However, if a category is supplied, we should get a filtered list of photos in the same category:

```
query {
    allPhotos(category: "SELFIE") {
        name
        description
        url
    }
}
```

This query would return the `name`, `description`, and `url` of every photo categorized as a `SELFIE`.

Data paging

If our PhotoShare application is successful, which it will be, it will have a lot of `Users` and `Photos`. Returning every `User` or every `Photo` in our application might not be possible. We can use GraphQL arguments to control the amount of data that is returned from our queries. This process is called *data paging* because a specific number of records are returned to represent one page of data.

To implement data paging, we are going to add two optional arguments: `first` to collect the number of records that should be returned at once in a single data page, and `start` to define the starting position or index of the first record to return. We can add these arguments to both of our list queries:

```
type Query {
    ...
    allUsers(first: Int=50 start: Int=0): [User!]!
    allPhotos(first: Int=25 start: Int=0): [Photo!]!
}
```

In the preceding example, we have added optional arguments for `first` and `start`. If the client does not supply these arguments with the query, we will use the default values provided. By default, the `allUsers` query returns only the first 50 users, and the `allPhotos` query returns only the first 25 photos.

The client can query a different range of either user or photos by supplying values for these arguments. For example, if we want to select users 90 through 100, we could do so by using the following query:

```
query {
    allUsers(first: 10 start: 90) {
        name
        avatar
```

```
        }
    }
```

This query selects only 10 years starting at the 90th user. It should return the name and avatar for that specific range of users. We can calculate the total number of pages that are available on the client by dividing the total number of items by the size of one page of data:

```
pages = pageSize/total
```

Sorting

When querying a list of data, we might also want to define how the returned list of data should be sorted. We can use arguments for this, as well.

Consider a scenario in which we wanted to incorporate the ability to sort any lists of Photo records. One way to tackle this challenge is to create enums that specify which fields can be used to sort Photo objects and instructions for how to sort those fields:

```
enum SortDirection {
    ASCENDING
    DESCENDING
}

enum SortablePhotoField {
    name
    description
    category
    created
}

Query {
    allPhotos(
        sort: SortDirection = DESCENDING
        sortBy: SortablePhotoField = created
    ): [Photo!]!
}
```

Here, we've added the arguments sort and sortBy to the allPhotos query. We created an enumeration type called SortDirection that we can use to limit the values of the sort argument to ASCENDING or DESCENDING. We've also created another enumeration type for SortablePhotoField. We don't want to sort photos on just any field, so we've restricted sortBy values to include only four of the photo fields: name, description, category, or created (the date and time that the photo was added). Both sort and sortBy are optional arguments, so they default to DESCENDING and created if either of the arguments are not supplied.

Clients can now control how their photos are sorted when they issue an `allPhotos` query:

```
query {
    allPhotos(sortBy: name)
}
```

This query will return all of the photos sorted by descending name.

So far, we've added arguments only to fields of the `Query` type, but it is important to note that you can add arguments to any field. We could add the filtering, sorting, and paging arguments to the photos that have been posted by a single user:

```
type User {
    postedPhotos(
        first: Int = 25
        start: Int = 0
        sort: SortDirection = DESCENDING
        sortBy: SortablePhotoField = created
        category: PhotoCategory
    ): [Photo!]
```

Adding pagination filters can help reduce the amount of data a query can return. We discuss the idea of limiting data at greater length in Chapter 7.

Mutations

Mutations must be defined in the schema. Just like queries, mutations also are defined in their own custom object type and added to the schema. Technically, there is no difference between how a mutation or query is defined in your schema. The difference is in intent. We should create mutations only when an action or event will change something about the state of our application.

Mutations should represent the *verbs* in your application. They should consist of the things that users should be able to *do* with your service. When designing your GraphQL service, make a list of all of the actions that a user can take with your application. Those are most likely your mutations.

In the PhotoShare app, users can sign in with GitHub, post photos, and tag photos. All of these actions change something about the state of the application. After they are signed in with GitHub, the current users accessing the client will change. When a user posts a photo, there will be an additional photo in the system. The same is true for tagging photos. New photo-tag data records are generated each time a photo is tagged.

We can add these mutations to our root mutation type in our schema and make them available to the client. Let's begin with our first mutation, `postPhoto`:

```
type Mutation {
    postPhoto(
        name: String!
        description: String
        category: PhotoCategory=PORTRAIT
    ): Photo!
}

schema {
    query: Query
    mutation: Mutation
}
```

Adding a field under the `Mutation` type called `postPhoto` makes it possible for users to post photos. Well, at least it makes it possible for users to post metadata about photos. We handle uploading the actual photos in Chapter 7.

When a user posts a photo, at a bare minimum the photo's `name` is required. The `description` and `category` are optional. If a `category` argument is not supplied, the posted photo will be defaulted to `PORTRAIT`. For example, a user can post a photo by sending the following mutation:

```
mutation {
    postPhoto(name: "Sending the Palisades") {
        id
        url
        created
        postedBy {
            name
        }
    }
}
```

After the user posts a photo, they can select information about the photo that they just posted. This is good because some of the record details about the new photo will be generated on the server. The `ID` for our new photo will be created by the database. The photo's `url` will automatically be generated. The photo will also be timestamped with the date and time that the photo was `created`. This query selects all of these new fields after a photo has been posted.

Additionally, the selection set includes information about the user who posted the photo. A user must be signed in to post a photo. If no user is presently signed in, this mutation should return an error. Assuming that a user is signed in, we can obtain details about who posted the photo via the `postedBy` field. In Chapter 5, we cover how to authenticate an authorized user by using an access token.

Input Types

As you might have noticed, the arguments for a couple of our queries and mutations are getting quite lengthy. There is a better way to organize these arguments using *input types*. An input type is similar to the GraphQL object type except it is used only for input arguments.

Let's improve the postPhoto mutation using an input type for our arguments:

```
input PostPhotoInput {
  name: String!
  description: String
  category: PhotoCategory=PORTRAIT
}

type Mutation {
    postPhoto(input: PostPhotoInput!): Photo!
}
```

The PostPhotoInput type is like an object type, but it was created only for input arguments. It requires a name and the description, but category fields are still optional. Now when sending the postPhoto mutation, the details about the new photo need to be included in one object:

```
mutation newPhoto($input: PostPhotoInput!) {
    postPhoto(input: $input) {
```

```
            id
            url
            created
        }
    }
```

When we create this mutation, we set the `$input` query variable's type to match our `PostPhotoInput!` input type. It is non-nullable because at minimum we need to access the `input.name` field to add a new photo. When we send the mutation, we need to supply the new photo data in our query variables nested under the `input` field:

```
{
    "input": {
        "name": "Hanging at the Arc",
        "description": "Sunny on the deck of the Arc",
        "category": "LANDSCAPE"
    }
}
```

Our input is grouped together in a JSON object and sent along with the mutation in the query variables under the "input" key. Because the query variables are formatted as JSON, the category needs to be a string that matches one of the categories from the `PhotoCategory` type.

Input types are key to organizing and writing a clear GraphQL schema. You can use input types as arguments on any field. You can use them to improve both data paging and data filtering in applications.

Let's take a look at how we can organize and reuse all of our sorting and filtering fields by using input types:

```
input PhotoFilter {
    category: PhotoCategory
    createdBetween: DateRange
    taggedUsers: [ID!]
    searchText: String
}

input DateRange {
    start: DateTime!
    end: DateTime!
}

input DataPage {
    first: Int = 25
    start: Int = 0
}

input DataSort {
    sort: SortDirection = DESCENDING
```

```
        sortBy: SortablePhotoField = created
}

type User {
    ...
    postedPhotos(filter:PhotoFilter paging:DataPage sorting:DataSort): [Photo!]!
    inPhotos(filter:PhotoFilter paging:DataPage sorting:DataSort): [Photo!]!
}

type Photo {
    ...
    taggedUsers(sorting:DataSort): [User!]!
}

type Query {
    ...
    allUsers(paging:DataPage sorting:DataSort): [User!]!
    allPhotos(filter:PhotoFilter paging:DataPage sorting:DataSort): [Photo!]!
}
```

We've organized numerous fields under input types and have reused those fields as arguments across our schema.

The PhotoFilter input types contain optional input fields that allow the client to filter a list of photos. The PhotoFilter type includes a nested input type, DateRange, under the field createdBetween. DateRange must include start and end dates. Using the PhotoFilter, we also can filter photos by category, search string, or taggedUsers. We add all of these filter options to every field that returns a list of photos. This gives the client a lot of control over which photos are returned from every list.

Input types have also been created for paging and sorting. The DataPage input type contains the fields needed to request a page of data and the DataSort input type contains our sorting fields. These input types have been added to every field in our schema that returns a list of data.

We could write a query that accepts some pretty complex input data using the available input types:

```
query getPhotos($filter:PhotoFilter $page:DataPage $sort:DataSort) {
    allPhotos(filter:$filter paging:$page sorting:$sort) {
        id
        name
        url
    }
}
```

This query optionally accepts arguments for three input types: $filter, $page, and $sort. Using query variables, we can send some specific details about what photos we would like to return:

```
{
    "filter": {
        "category": "ACTION",
        "taggedUsers": ["MoonTahoe", "EvePorcello"],
        "createdBetween": {
            "start": "2018-11-6",
            "end": "2018-5-31"
        }
    },
    "page": {
        "first": 100
    }
}
```

This query will find all of the ACTION photos for which GitHub users MoonTahoe and EvePorcello are tagged between November 6th and May 31st, which happens to be ski season. We also ask for the first 100 photos with this query.

Input types help us organize our schema and reuse arguments. They also improve the schema documentation that GraphiQL or GraphQL Playground automatically generates. This will make your API more approachable and easier to learn and digest. Finally, you can use input types to give the client a lot of power to execute organized queries.

Return Types

All of the fields in our schema have been returning our main types, User and Photo. But sometimes we need to return meta information about queries and mutations in addition to the actual payload data. For example, when a user has signed in and been authenticated, we need to return a token in addition to the User payload.

To sign in with GitHub OAuth, we must obtain an OAuth code from GitHub. We discuss setting up your own GitHub OAuth account and obtaining the GitHub code in "GitHub Authorization" on page 107. For now, let's assume that you have a valid Git-Hub code that you can send to the githubAuth mutation to sign in a user:

```
type AuthPayload {
    user: User!
    token: String!
}

type Mutation {
    ...
    githubAuth(code: String!): AuthPayload!
}
```

Users are authenticated by sending a valid GitHub code to the githubAuth mutation. If successful, we will return a custom object type that contains both information about the user that was successfully signed in as well as a token that can be used to authorize further queries and mutations including the `postPhoto` mutation.

You can use custom return types on any field for which we need more than simple payload data. Maybe we want to know how long it takes for a query to deliver a response, or how many results were found in a particular response in addition to the query payload data. You can handle all of this by using a custom return type.

At this point, we have introduced all of the types that are available to you when creating GraphQL schemas. We've even taken a bit of time to discuss techniques that can help you improve your schema design. But there is one last root object type that we need to introduce—the `Subscription` type.

Subscriptions

`Subscription` types are no different than any other object type in the GraphQL schema definition language. Here, we define the available subscriptions as fields on a custom object type. It will be up to us to make sure the subscriptions implement the PubSub design pattern along with some sort of real-time transport when we build the GraphQL service later in Chapter 7.

For example, we can add subscriptions that allow our clients to listen for the creation of new `Photo` or `User` types:

```
type Subscription {
    newPhoto: Photo!
    newUser: User!
}

schema {
    query: Query
    mutation: Mutation
    subscription: Subscription
}
```

Here, we create a custom `Subscription` object that contains two fields: `newPhoto` and `newUser`. When a new photo is posted, that new photo will be pushed to all of the clients who have subscribed to the `newPhoto` subscription. When a new user has been created, their details are pushed to every client who is listening for new users.

Just like queries or mutations, subscriptions can take advantage of arguments. Suppose that we want to add filters to the `newPhoto` subscription that would cause it to listen only for new `ACTION` photos:

```
type Subscription {
    newPhoto(category: PhotoCategory): Photo!
```

```
        newUser: User!
    }
```

When users subscribe to the `newPhoto` subscription, they now have the option to filter the photos that are pushed to this subscription. For example, to filter for only new `ACTION` photos, clients could send the following operation to our GraphQL API:

```
subscription {
    newPhoto(category: "ACTION") {
        id
        name
        url
        postedBy {
            name
        }
    }
}
```

This subscription should return details for only `ACTION` photos.

A subscription is a great solution when it's important to handle data in real time. In Chapter 7, we talk more about subscription implementation for all of your real-time data handling needs.

Schema Documentation

Chapter 3 explains how GraphQL has an introspection system that can inform you as to what queries the server supports. When writing a GraphQL schema, you can add optional descriptions for each field that will provide additional information about the schema's types and fields. Providing descriptions can make it easier for your team, yourself, and other users of the API to understand your type system.

For example, let's add comments to the `User` type in our schema:

```
"""
A user who has been authorized by GitHub at least once
"""
type User {

    """
    The user's unique GitHub login
    """
    githubLogin: ID!

    """
    The user's first and last name
    """
    name: String

    """
    A url for the user's GitHub profile photo
```

```
"""
avatar: String

"""
All of the photos posted by this user
"""
postedPhotos: [Photo!]!

"""
All of the photos in which this user appears
"""
inPhotos: [Photo!]!

}
```

By adding three quotation marks above and below your comment on each type or field, you provide users with a dictionary for your API. In addition to types and fields, you can also document arguments. Let's look at the postPhoto mutation:

```
Replace with:

type Mutation {
  """
  Authorizes a GitHub User
  """
  githubAuth(
    "The unique code from GitHub that is sent to authorize the user"
    code: String!
  ): AuthPayload!
}
```

The argument comments share the name of the argument and whether the field is optional. If you're using input types, you can document these like any other type:

```
"""
The inputs sent with the postPhoto Mutation
"""
input PostPhotoInput {
  "The name of the new photo"
  name: String!
  "(optional) A brief description of the photo"
  description: String
  "(optional) The category that defines the photo"
  category: PhotoCategory=PORTRAIT
}

postPhoto(
    "input: The name, description, and category for a new photo"
    input: PostPhotoInput!
): Photo!
```

All of these documentation notes are then listed in the schema documentation in the GraphQL Playground or GraphiQL as shown in Figure 4-4. Of course, you can also issue introspection queries to find the descriptions of these types.

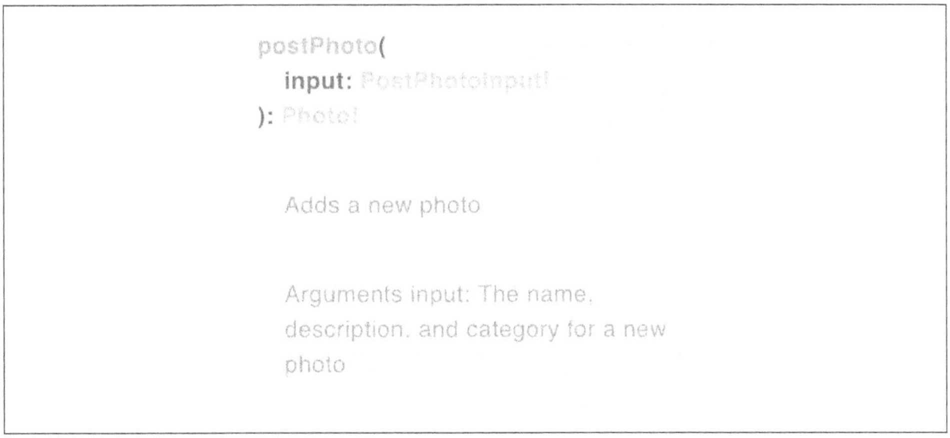

Figure 4-4. postPhoto Documentation

At the heart of all GraphQL projects is a solid, well-defined schema. This serves as a roadmap and a contract between the frontend and backend teams to ensure that the product built always serves the schema.

In this chapter, we created a schema for our photo-sharing application. In the next three chapters, we show you how to build a full-stack GraphQL application that fulfills the contract of the schema we just created.

CHAPTER 5

Creating a GraphQL API

You explored the history. You wrote some queries. You created a schema. Now you're ready to create a fully functioning GraphQL service. This can be done with a range of different technologies, but we're going to use JavaScript. The techniques that are shared here are fairly universal, so even if the implementation details differ, the overall architecture will be similar no matter which language or framework you choose.

If you are interested in server libraries for other languages, you can check out the many that exist at GraphQL.org (*http://graphql.org/code/*).

When the GraphQL spec was released in 2015, it focused on a clear explanation of the query language and type system. It intentionally left details about server implementation more vague to allow developers from a variety of language backgrounds to use what was comfortable for them. The team at Facebook did provide a reference implementation that they built in JavaScript called GraphQL.js. Along with this, they released *express-graphql*, a simple way to create a GraphQL server with Express, and notably, the first library to help developers accomplish this task.

After our exploration of JavaScript implementations of GraphQL servers, we've chosen to use Apollo Server (*https://www.apollographql.com/docs/apollo-server/v2/*), an open-source solution from the Apollo team. Apollo Server is fairly simple to set up and offers an array of production-ready features including subscription support, file uploads, a data source API for quickly hooking up existing services, and Apollo Engine integration out of the box. It also includes GraphQL Playground for writing queries directly in the browser.

Project Setup

Let's begin by creating the `photo-share-api` project as an empty folder on your computer. Remember: you can always visit the *Learning GraphQL* repo (*https://*

github.com/MoonHighway/learning-graphql/tree/master/chapter-05/photo-share-api/)
to see the completed project or to see the project running on Glitch. From within that
folder, we'll generate a new npm project using the `npm init -y` command in your
Terminal or Command Prompt. This utility will generate a `package.json` file and set
all of the options as the default, since we used the `-y` flag.

Next, we'll install the project dependencies: `apollo-server` and `graphql`. We'll also
install `nodemon`:

```
npm install apollo-server graphql nodemon
```

`apollo-server` and `graphql` are required to set up an instance of Apollo Server. `node
mon` will watch files for changes and restart the server when we make changes. This
way, we won't have to stop and restart the server every time we make a change. Let's
add the command for `nodemon` to the package.json on the `scripts` key:

```
"scripts": {
  "start": "nodemon -e js,json,graphql"
}
```

Now every time we run `npm start`, our `index.js` file will run and `nodemon` will watch
for changes in any files with a `js`, `json`, or `graphql` extension. Also, we want to create
an `index.js` file at the root of the project. Be sure that the `main` file in the `pack
age.json` is pointing to `index.js`:

```
"main": "index.js"
```

Resolvers

In our discussion of GraphQL so far, we've focused a lot on queries. A schema defines
the query operations that clients are allowed to make and also how different types are
related. A schema describes the data requirements but doesn't perform the work of
getting that data. That work is handled by resolvers.

A *resolver* is a function that returns data for a particular field. Resolver functions
return data in the type and shape specified by the schema. Resolvers can be asynchronous and can fetch or update data from a REST API, database, or any other service.

Let's take a look at what a resolver might look like for our root query. In our `index.js`
file at the root of the project, let's add the `totalPhotos` field to the `Query`:

```
const typeDefs = `
    type Query {
        totalPhotos: Int!
    }
`

const resolvers = {
  Query: {
```

```
        totalPhotos: () => 42
    }
}
```

The `typeDefs` variable is where we define our schema. It's just a string. Whenever we create a query like `totalPhotos`, it should be backed by a resolver function of the same name. The type definition describes which type the field should return. The resolver function returns the data of that type from somewhere—in this case, just a static value of 42.

It is also important to note that the resolver must be defined under an object with the same `typename` as the object in the schema. The `totalPhotos` field is a part of the query object. The resolver for this field must also be a part of the `Query` object.

We have created initial type definitions for our root query. We've also created our first resolver that backs the `totalPhotos` query field. To create the schema and enable the execution of queries against the schema, we will use Apollo Server:

```
// 1. Require 'apollo-server'
const { ApolloServer } = require('apollo-server')

const typeDefs = `
        type Query {
                totalPhotos: Int!
        }
    `

const resolvers = {
  Query: {
    totalPhotos: () => 42
  }
}

// 2. Create a new instance of the server.
// 3. Send it an object with typeDefs (the schema) and resolvers
const server = new ApolloServer({
  typeDefs,
  resolvers
})


// 4. Call listen on the server to launch the web server
server
  .listen()
  .then(({url}) => console.log(`GraphQL Service running on ${url}`))
```

After requiring `ApolloServer`, we'll create a new instance of the server, sending it an object with two values: `typeDefs` and `resolvers`. This is a quick and minimal server setup that still allows us to stand up a powerful GraphQL API. Later in the chapter, we will talk about how to extend the functionality of the server using Express.

At this point, we are ready to execute a query for `totalPhotos`. Once we run `npm start`, we should see the GraphQL Playground running on `http://localhost:4000`. Let's try the following query:

```
{
    totalPhotos
}
```

The returned data for `totalPhotos` is 42 as expected:

```
{
  "data": {
    "totalPhotos": 42
  }
}
```

Resolvers are key to the implementation of GraphQL. Every field must have a corresponding resolver function. The resolver must follow the rules of the schema. It must have the same name as the field that was defined in the schema, and it must return the datatype defined by the schema.

Root Resolvers

As discussed in Chapter 4, GraphQL APIs have root types for `Query`, `Mutation`, and `Subscription`. These types are found at the top level and represent all of the possible entry points into the API. So far, we've added the `totalPhotos` field to the `Query` type, meaning that our API can query this field.

Let's add to this by creating a root type for `Mutation`. The mutation field is called `postPhoto` and will take in a `name` and `description` as arguments of the type `String`. When the mutation is sent, it must return a `Boolean`:

```
const typeDefs = `
    type Query {
        totalPhotos: Int!
    }

    type Mutation {
        postPhoto(name: String! description: String): Boolean!
    }
`
```

After we create the `postPhoto` mutation, we need to add a corresponding resolver in the `resolvers` object:

```
// 1. A data type to store our photos in memory
var photos = []
```

```
const resolvers = {
  Query: {

    // 2. Return the length of the photos array
    totalPhotos: () => photos.length

  },

  // 3. Mutation and postPhoto resolver
  Mutation: {
    postPhoto(parent, args) {
        photos.push(args)
        return true
    }
  }

}
```

First, we need to create a variable called photos to store the photo details in an array. Later on in this chapter, we will store photos in a database.

Next, we enhance the totalPhotos resolver to return the length of the photos array. Whenever this field is queried, it will return the number of photos that are presently stored in the array.

From here, we add the postPhoto resolver. This time, we are using function arguments with our postPhoto function. The first argument is a reference to the parent object. Sometimes you'll see this represented as _, root, or obj in documentation. In this case, the parent of the postPhoto resolver is a Mutation. The parent does not currently contain any data that we need to use, but it is always the first argument sent to a resolver. Therefore, we need to add a placeholder parent argument so that we can access the second argument sent to the resolver: the mutation arguments.

The second argument sent to the postPhoto resolver is the GraphQL arguments that were sent to this operation: the name and, optionally, the description. The args variable is an object that contains these two fields: {name,description}. Right now, the arguments represent one photo object, so we push them directly into the photos array.

It's now time to test the postPhoto mutation in GraphQL Playground, sending a string for the name argument:

```
mutation newPhoto {
    postPhoto(name: "sample photo")
}
```

This mutation adds the photo details to the array and returns true. Let's modify this mutation to use query variables:

```
    mutation newPhoto($name: String!, $description: String) {
        postPhoto(name: $name, description: $description)
    }
```

After variables are added to the mutation, data must be passed to provide the string variables. In the lower-left corner of the Playground, let's add values for name and description to the Query Variables window:

```
{
    "name": "sample photo A",
    "description": "A sample photo for our dataset"
}
```

Type Resolvers

When a GraphQL query, mutation, or subscription is executed, it returns a result that is the same shape of the query. We've seen how resolvers can return scalar type values like integers, strings, and Booleans, but resolvers can also return objects.

For our photo app, let's create a Photo type and an allPhotos query field that will return a list of Photo objects:

```
const typeDefs = `

    # 1. Add Photo type definition
    type Photo {
      id: ID!
      url: String!
      name: String!
      description: String
    }

    # 2. Return Photo from allPhotos
    type Query {
      totalPhotos: Int!
      allPhotos: [Photo!]!
    }

    # 3. Return the newly posted photo from the mutation
    type Mutation {
      postPhoto(name: String! description: String): Photo!
    }
    `
```

Because we've added the Photo object and the allPhotos query to our type definitions, we need reflect these adjustments in the resolvers. The postPhoto mutation needs to return data in the shape of the Photo type. The query allPhotos needs to return a list of objects that have the same shape as the Photo type:

```
// 1. A variable that we will increment for unique ids
var _id = 0
```

```
var photos = []

const resolvers = {
  Query: {
    totalPhotos: () => photos.length,
    allPhotos: () => photos
  },
  Mutation: {
    postPhoto(parent, args) {

      // 2. Create a new photo, and generate an id
        var newPhoto = {
          id: _id++,
          ...args
      }
      photos.push(newPhoto)

      // 3. Return the new photo
      return newPhoto

    }
  }
}
```

Because the Photo type requires an ID, we created a variable to store the ID. In the postPhoto resolver, we will generate IDs by incrementing this value. The args variable provides the name and description fields for the photo, but we also need an ID. It is typically up to the server to create variables like identifiers and timestamps. So, when we create a new photo object in the postPhoto resolver, we add the ID field and spread the name and description fields from args into our new photo object.

Instead of returning a Boolean, the mutation returns an object that matches the shape of the Photo type. This object is constructed with the generated ID and the name and description fields that were passed in with data. Additionally, the postPhoto mutation adds photo objects to the photos array. These objects match the shape of the Photo type that we defined in our schema, so we can return the entire array of photos from the allPhotos query.

 Generating unique IDs with an incremented variable is clearly a very unscalable way to create IDs, but will serve our purposes here as a demonstration. In a real app, your ID would likely be generated by the database.

To verify that postPhoto is working correctly, we can adjust the mutation. Because Photo is a type, we need to add a selection set to our mutation:

```
mutation newPhoto($name: String!, $description: String) {
    postPhoto(name: $name, description: $description) {
```

```
            id
            name
            description
        }
    }
```

After adding a few photos via mutations, the following `allPhotos` query should return an array of all of the Photo objects added:

```
query listPhotos {
    allPhotos {
        id
        name
        description
    }
}
```

We also added a non-nullable `url` field to our photo schema. What happens when we add a `url` to our selection set?

```
query listPhotos {
    allPhotos {
        id
        name
        description
        url
    }
}
```

When `url` is added to our query's selection set, an error is displayed: `Cannot return null for non-nullable field Photo.url`. We do not add a `url` field in the dataset. We do not need to store URLs, because they can be automatically generated. Each field in our schema can map to a resolver. All we need to do is add a `Photo` object to our list of resolvers and define the fields that we want to map to functions. In this case, we want to use a function to help us resolve URLs:

```
const resolvers = {
  Query: { ... },
  Mutation: { ... },
  Photo: {
    url: parent => `http://yoursite.com/img/${parent.id}.jpg`
  }
}
```

Because we are going to use a resolver for photo URLs, we've added a `Photo` object to our resolvers. This `Photo` resolver added to the root is called a *trivial resolver*. Trivial resolvers are added to the top level of the `resolvers` object, but they are not required. We have the option to create custom resolvers for the `Photo` object using a trivial resolver. If you do not specify a trivial resolver, GraphQL will fall back to a default resolver that returns a property as the same name as the field.

When we select a photo's `url` in our query, the corresponding resolver function is invoked. The first argument sent to resolvers is always the `parent` object. In this case, the `parent` represents the current `Photo` object that is being resolved. We're assuming here that our service handles only JPEG images. Those images are named by their photo ID and can be found on the `http://yoursite.com/img/` route. Because the `parent` is the photo, we can obtain the photo's ID through this argument and use it to automatically generate a URL for the current photo.

When we define a GraphQL schema, we describe the data requirements of our application. With resolvers, we can powerfully and flexibly fulfill those requirements. Functions give us this power and flexibility. Functions can be asynchronous, can return scalar types and return objects, and can return data from various sources. Resolvers are just functions, and every field in our GraphQL schema can map to a resolver.

Using Inputs and Enums

It's time to introduce an enumeration type, `PhotoCategory`, and an input type, `Post PhotoInput`, to our `typeDefs`:

```
enum PhotoCategory {
  SELFIE
  PORTRAIT
  ACTION
  LANDSCAPE
  GRAPHIC
}

type Photo {
  ...
  category: PhotoCategory!
}

input PostPhotoInput {
  name: String!
  category: PhotoCategory=PORTRAIT
  description: String
}

type Mutation {
  postPhoto(input: PostPhotoInput!): Photo!
}
```

In Chapter 4, we created these types when we designed the schema for the Photo-Share application. We also added the `PhotoCategory` enumeration type and added a `category` field to our photos. When resolving photos, we need to make sure that the photo category—a string that matches the values defined in the enumeration type—is available. We also need to collect a category when users post new photos.

We've added a `PostPhotoInput` type to organize the argument for the `postPhoto` mutation under a single object. This input type has a category field. Even when a user does not supply a category field as an argument, the default, `PORTRAIT`, will be used.

For the `postPhoto` resolver, we need to make some adjustments, as well. The details for the photo, the `name`, `description`, and `category` are now nested within the `input` field. We need to make sure that we access these values at `args.input` instead of `args`:

```
postPhoto(parent, args) {
    var newPhoto = {
        id: _id++,
        ...args.input
    }
    photos.push(newPhoto)
    return newPhoto
}
```

Now, we run the mutation with the new input type:

```
mutation newPhoto($input: PostPhotoInput!) {
  postPhoto(input:$input) {
    id
    name
    url
    description
    category
  }
}
```

We also need to send the corresponding JSON in the Query Variables panel:

```
{
  "input": {
    "name": "sample photo A",
    "description": "A sample photo for our dataset"
  }
}
```

If the category is not supplied, it will default to `PORTRAIT`. Alternatively, if a value is provided for `category`, it will be validated against our enumeration type before the operation is even sent to the server. If it's a valid category, it will be passed to the resolver as an argument.

With input types, we can make passing arguments to mutations more reusable and less error-prone. When combining input types and enums, we can be more specific about the types of inputs that can be supplied to specific fields. Inputs and enums are incredibly valuable and are made even better when you use them together.

Edges and Connections

As we've discussed previously, the power of GraphQL comes from the edges: the connections between data points. When standing up a GraphQL server, types typically map to models. Think of these types as being saved in tables of like data. From there, we link types with connections. Let's explore the kinds of connections that we can use to define the interconnected relationships between types.

One-to-many connections

Users need to access the list of photos they previously posted. We will access this data on a field called postedPhotos that will resolve to a filtered list of photos that the user has posted. Because one User can post many Photos, we call this a *one-to-many relationship*. Let's add the User to our typeDefs:

```
type User {
  githubLogin: ID!
  name: String
  avatar: String
  postedPhotos: [Photo!]!
}
```

At this point, we've created a directed graph. We can traverse from the User type to the Photo type. To have an undirected graph, we need to provide a way back to the User type from the Photo type. Let's add a postedBy field to the Photo type:

```
type Photo {
  id: ID!
  url: String!
  name: String!
  description: String
  category: PhotoCategory!
  postedBy: User!
}
```

By adding the postedBy field, we have created a link back to the User who posted the Photo, creating an undirected graph. This is a *one-to-one connection* because one photo can only be posted by one User.

> ### Sample Users
>
> To test our server, let's add some sample data to our index.js file. Be sure to remove the current photos variable that is set to an empty array:
>
> ```
> var users = [
>   { "githubLogin": "mHattrup", "name": "Mike Hattrup" },
>   { "githubLogin": "gPlake", "name": "Glen Plake" },
>   { "githubLogin": "sSchmidt", "name": "Scot Schmidt" }
> ]
> ```

```
var photos = [
  {
    "id": "1",
    "name": "Dropping the Heart Chute",
    "description": "The heart chute is one of my favorite chutes",
    "category": "ACTION",
    "githubUser": "gPlake"
  },
  {
    "id": "2",
    "name": "Enjoying the sunshine",
    "category": "SELFIE",
    "githubUser": "sSchmidt"
  },
  {
    id: "3",
    "name": "Gunbarrel 25",
    "description": "25 laps on gunbarrel today",
    "category": "LANDSCAPE",
    "githubUser": "sSchmidt"
  }
]
```

Because connections are created using the fields of an object type, they can map to resolver functions. Inside these functions, we can use the details about the parent to help us locate and return the connected data.

Let's add the postedPhotos and postedBy resolvers to our service:

```
const resolvers = {
  ...
  Photo: {
    url: parent => `http://yoursite.com/img/${parent.id}.jpg`,
    postedBy: parent => {
      return users.find(u => u.githubLogin === parent.githubUser)
    }
  },
  User: {
    postedPhotos: parent => {
      return photos.filter(p => p.githubUser === parent.githubLogin)
    }
  }
}
```

In the Photo resolver, we need to add a field for postedBy. Within this resolver, it's up to us to figure out how to find the connected data. Using the .find() array method, we can obtain the user who's githubLogin matches the githubUser value saved with each photo. The .find() method returns a single user object.

In the User resolver, we retrieve a list of photos posted by that user using the array's `.filter()` method. This method returns an array of only those photos that contain a githubUser value that matches the parent user's githubLogin value. The filter method returns an array of photos.

Now let's try to send the allPhotos query:

```
query photos {
  allPhotos {
    name
    url
    postedBy {
      name
    }
  }
}
```

When we query each photo, we are able to query the user who posted that photo. The user object is being located and returned by the resolver. In this example, we select only the name of the user who posted the photo. Given our sample data, the result should return the following JSON:

```
{
  "data": {
    "allPhotos": [
      {
        "name": "Dropping the Heart Chute",
        "url": "http://yoursite.com/img/1.jpg",
        "postedBy": {
          "name": "Glen Plake"
        }
      },
      {
        "name": "Enjoying the sunshine",
        "url": "http://yoursite.com/img/2.jpg",
        "postedBy": {
          "name": "Scot Schmidt"
        }
      },
      {
        "name": "Gunbarrel 25",
        "url": "http://yoursite.com/img/3.jpg",
        "postedBy": {
          "name": "Scot Schmidt"
        }
      }
    ]
  }
}
```

We are responsible for connecting the data with resolvers, but as soon as we are able to return that connected data, our clients can begin writing powerful queries. In the next section, we show you some techniques to create many-to-many connections.

Many-to-many

The next feature we want to add to our service is the ability to tag users in photos. This means that a User could be tagged in many different photos, and Photo could have many different users tagged in it. The relationship that photo tags will create between users and photos can be referred to as *many-to-many*—many users to many photos.

To facilitate the many-to-many relationship, we add the taggedUsers field to Photo and a inPhotos field to User. Let's modify the typeDefs:

```
type User {
    ...
    inPhotos: [Photo!]!
}

type Photo {
    ...
    taggedUsers: [User!]!
}
```

The taggedUsers field returns a list of users, and the inPhotos field returns a list of photos in which a user appears. To facilitate this many-to-many connection, we need to add a tags array. To test the tagging feature, you need to populate some sample data for tags:

```
var tags = [
    { "photoID": "1", "userID": "gPlake" },
    { "photoID": "2", "userID": "sSchmidt" },
    { "photoID": "2", "userID": "mHattrup" },
    { "photoID": "2", "userID": "gPlake" }
]
```

When we have a photo, we must search our datasets to find the users who have been tagged in the photo. When we have a user, it is up to us to find the list of photos in which that user appears. Because our data is currently stored in JavaScript arrays, we will use array methods within the resolvers to find the data:

```
Photo: {
    ...
    taggedUsers: parent => tags

        // Returns an array of tags that only contain the current photo
        .filter(tag => tag.photoID === parent.id)

        // Converts the array of tags into an array of userIDs
```

```
        .map(tag => tag.userID)

      // Converts array of userIDs into an array of user objects
      .map(userID => users.find(u => u.githubLogin === userID))

  },
  User: {
    ...
    inPhotos: parent => tags

      // Returns an array of tags that only contain the current user
      .filter(tag => tag.userID === parent.id)

      // Converts the array of tags into an array of photoIDs
      .map(tag => tag.photoID)

      // Converts array of photoIDs into an array of photo objects
      .map(photoID => photos.find(p => p.id === photoID))

  }
```

The taggedUsers field resolver filters out any photos that are not the current photo
and maps that filtered list to an array of actual User objects. The inPhotos field
resolver filters the tags by user and maps the user tags to an array of actual Photo
objects.

We can now view which users are tagged in every photo by sending a GraphQL
query:

```
query listPhotos {
  allPhotos {
    url
    taggedUsers {
      name
    }
  }
}
```

You might have noticed that we have an array for tags, but we do not have a
GraphQL type called Tag. GraphQL does not require our data models to exactly
match the types in our schema. Our clients can find the tagged users in every photo
and the photos that any users are tagged in by querying the User type or the Photo
type. They don't need to query a Tag type: that would just complicate things. We've
already done the heavy lifting of finding the tagged users or photos in our resolver
specifically to make it easy for clients to query this data.

Custom Scalars

As discussed in Chapter 4, GraphQL has a collection of default scalar types that you
can use for any fields. Scalars like Int, Float, String, Boolean, and ID are suitable for

the majority of situations, but there might be instances for which you need to create a custom scalar type to suit your data requirements.

When we implement a custom scalar, we need to create rules around how the type should be serialized and validated. For example, if we create a DateTime type, we will need to define what should be considered a valid DateTime.

Let's add this custom DateTime scalar to our typeDefs and use it in the Photo type for the created field. The created field is used to store the date and time at which a specific photo was posted:

```
const typeDefs = `
  scalar DateTime
  type Photo {
    ...
    created: DateTime!
  }
  ...
`
```

Every field in our schema needs to map to a resolver. The created field needs to map to a resolver for the DateTime type. We created a custom scalar type for DateTime because we want to parse and validate any fields that use this scalar as JavaScript Date types.

Consider the various ways in which we can represent a date and time as a string. All of these strings represent valid dates:

- "4/18/2018"
- "4/18/2018 1:30:00 PM"
- "Sun Apr 15 2018 12:10:17 GMT-0700 (PDT)"
- "2018-04-15T19:09:57.308Z"

We can use any of these strings to create datetime objects with JavaScript:

```
var d = new Date("4/18/2018")
console.log( d.toISOString() )
// "2018-04-18T07:00:00.000Z"
```

Here, we created a new date object using one format and then converted that date time string into an ISO-formatted date string.

Anything that the JavaScript Date object does not understand is invalid. You can try to parse the following data:

```
var d = new Date("Tuesday March")
console.log( d.toString() )
// "Invalid Date"
```

When we query the photo's `created` field, we want to make sure that the value returned by this field contains a string in the ISO date-time format. Whenever a field returns a date value, we `serialize` that value as an ISO-formatted string:

```
const serialize = value => new Date(value).toISOString()
```

The serialize function obtains the field values from our object, and as long as that field contains a date formatted as a JavaScript object or any valid `datetime` string, it will always be returned by GraphQL in the ISO `datetime` format.

When your schema implements a custom scalar, it can be used as an argument in a query. Let's assume that we created a filter for the `allPhotos` query. This query would return a list of photos taken after a specific date:

```
type Query {
  ...
  allPhotos(after: DateTime): [Photo!]!
}
```

If we had this field, clients could send us a query that contains a `DateTime` value:

```
query recentPhotos(after:DateTime) {
  allPhotos(after: $after) {
    name
    url
  }
}
```

And they would send the `$after` argument using query variables:

```
{
  "after": "4/18/2018"
}
```

We want to make sure that the `after` argument is parsed into a JavaScript `Date` object before it is sent to the resolver:

```
const parseValue = value => new Date(value)
```

We can use the `parseValue` function to parse the values of incoming strings that are sent along with queries. Whatever `parseValue` returns is passed to the resolver arguments:

```
const resolvers = {
  Query: {
    allPhotos: (parent, args) => {
      args.after // JavaScript Date Object
      ...
    }
```

```
    }
  }
```

Custom scalars need to be able to serialize and parse date values. There is one more place that we need to handle date strings. This is when clients add the date string directly to the query itself:

```
query {
  allPhotos(after: "4/18/2018") {
    name
    url
  }
}
```

The `after` argument is not being passed as a query variable. Instead, it has been added directly to the query document. Before we can parse this value, we need to obtain it from the query after it has been parsed into an abstract syntax tree (AST). We use the `parseLiteral` function to obtain these values from the query document before they are parsed:

```
const parseLiteral = ast => ast.value
```

The `parseLiteral` function is used to obtain the value of the date that was added directly to the query document. In this case, all we need to do is return that value, but if needed, we could take extra parsing steps inside this function.

We need all three of these functions that we designed to handle `DateTime` values when we create our custom scalar. Let's add the resolver for our custom `DateTime` scalar to our code:

```
const { GraphQLScalarType } = require('graphql')
...
const resolvers = {
  Query: { ... },
  Mutation: { ... },
  Photo: { ... },
  User: { ... },
  DateTime: new GraphQLScalarType({
      name: 'DateTime',
      description: 'A valid date time value.',
      parseValue: value => new Date(value),
      serialize: value => new Date(value).toISOString(),
      parseLiteral: ast => ast.value
  })
}
```

We use the `GraphQLScalarType` object to create resolvers for custom scalars. The `DateTime` resolver is placed within our list of resolvers. When creating a new scalar type, we need to add the three functions: `serialize`, `parseValue`, and `parseLiteral`, which will handle any fields or arguments that implement the `DateType` scalar.

Now, when we add `DateTime` fields to our selection sets, we can see those dates and types formatted as ISO date strings:

```
query listPhotos {
  allPhotos {
    name
    created
  }
}
```

The only thing left to do is make sure that we add a timestamp to each photo when it is posted. We do this by adding a `created` field to every photo and timestamping it with the current `DateTime` using the JavaScript `Date` object:

```
postPhoto(parent, args) {
    var newPhoto = {
        id: _id++,
        ...args.input,
        created: new Date()
    }
    photos.push(newPhoto)
    return newPhoto
}
```

Now, when new photos are posted, they will be timestamped with the date and time that they were created.

apollo-server-express

There might be a scenario where you want to add Apollo Server to an existing app, or you might want to take advantage of Express middleware. In that case, you might consider using `apollo-server-express`. With Apollo Server Express, you'll get to use all of the latest features of Apollo Server, but you'll also be able to set up a more custom configuration. For our purposes, we are going to refactor the server to use Apollo Server Express in order to set up a custom home route, a playground route, and later to allow for images that are posted to be uploaded and saved on the server.

Let's start by removing `apollo-server`:

```
npm remove apollo-server
```

Then, let's install Apollo Server Express and Express:

```
npm install apollo-server-express express
```

Express

Express is by far one of the most popular projects in the Node.js ecosystem. It allows you to set up a Node.js web application quickly and efficiently.

From here, we can refactor our `index.js` file. We'll start by changing the `require` statement to include `apollo-server-express`. Then we'll include `express`:

```
// 1. Require `apollo-server-express` and `express`
const { ApolloServer } = require('apollo-server-express')
const express = require('express')

...

// 2. Call `express()` to create an Express application
var app = express()

const server = new ApolloServer({ typeDefs, resolvers })

// 3. Call `applyMiddleware()` to allow middleware mounted on the same path
server.applyMiddleware({ app })

// 4. Create a home route
app.get('/', (req, res) => res.end('Welcome to the PhotoShare API'))

// 5. Listen on a specific port
app.listen({ port: 4000 }, () =>
  console.log(`GraphQL Server running @ http://localhost:4000${server.graphqlPath}`)
)
```

By including Express, we can take advantage of all of the middleware functions provided to us by the framework. To incorporate this into the server, we just need to call the express function, call applyMiddleware, and then we can set up a custom route. Now when we visit http://localhost:4000, we should see a page that reads "Welcome to the PhotoShare API". This is a placeholder for now.

Next, we want to set up a custom route for the GraphQL Playground to run at http://localhost:4000/playground. We can do so by installing a helper package from npm. First, we need to install the package, graphql-playground-middleware-express:

```
npm install graphql-playground-middleware-express
```

Then require this package at the top of the index file:

```
const expressPlayground = require('graphql-playground-middleware-express').default

...

app.get('/playground', expressPlayground({ endpoint: '/graphql' }))
```

Then we'll use Express to create a route for the Playground, so anytime we want to use the Playground, we'll visit http://localhost:4000/playground.

Now our server is set up with Apollo Server Express, and we have three distinct routes running:

- / for a homepage
- /graphql for the GraphQL endpoint
- /playground for the GraphQL Playground

At this point, we'll also reduce the length of our index file by moving the typeDefs and resolvers to their own files.

First, we'll create a file called typeDefs.graphql and place it at the root of the project. This will be just the schema, only text. You can also move the resolvers to their own folder called resolvers. You can place these functions in an index.js file, or you can modularize the resolver files as we do in the repository (*https://github.com/MoonHigh way/learning-graphql/tree/master/chapter-05/photo-share-api/resolvers*).

Once complete, you can import the typeDefs and resolvers as shown below. We'll use the fs module from Node.js to read the typeDefs.graphql file:

```
const { ApolloServer } = require('apollo-server-express')
const express = require('express')
const expressPlayground = require('graphql-playground-middleware-express').default
const { readFileSync } = require('fs')
```

```
const typeDefs = readFileSync('./typeDefs.graphql', 'UTF-8')
const resolvers = require('./resolvers')

var app = express()

const server = new ApolloServer({ typeDefs, resolvers })

server.applyMiddleware({ app })

app.get('/', (req, res) => res.end('Welcome to the PhotoShare API'))
app.get('/playground', expressPlayground({ endpoint: '/graphql' }))

app.listen({ port: 4000 }, () =>
  console.log(`GraphQL Server running at http://localhost:4000${server.graphqlPath}`)
)
```

Now that we've refactored the server, we're ready to take the next step: integrating a database.

Context

In this section, we take a look at *context*, which is the location where you can store global values that any resolver can access. Context is a good place to store authentication information, database details, local data caches, and anything else that is needed to resolve a GraphQL operation.

You can directly call REST APIs and databases in your resolvers, but we commonly abstract that logic into an object that we place on the context to enforce separation of concerns and allow for easier refactors later. You can also use context to access REST data from an Apollo Data Source. For more information on that, check out Apollo Data Sources in the documentation (*http://bit.ly/2vac9ZC*).

For our purposes here though, we are going to incorporate context now to address some of our app's current limitations. First of all, we're storing data in memory, which is not a very scalable solution. We are also handling IDs sloppily by incrementing these values with each mutation. Instead, we are going to rely on a database to handle data storage and ID generation. Our resolvers will be able to access this database from context.

Installing Mongo

GraphQL does not care what database you use. You can use Postgres, Mongo, SQL Server, Firebase, MySQL, Redis, Elastic—whatever you want. Due to its popularity among the Node.js community, we will use Mongo as the data storage solution for our application.

To get started with MongoDB on a Mac, we will use Homebrew. To install Homebrew, visit *https://brew.sh/*. After you have installed Homebrew, we will go through the process of installing Mongo with it by running the following commands:

```
brew install mongo
brew services list
brew services start
```

After you have successfully started MongoDB, we can start reading and writing data to the local Mongo instance.

Note for Windows Users

If you want to run a local version of MongoDB on Windows, check out *http://bit.ly/inst-mdb-windows*.

You can also use an online Mongo service like mLab, as pictured in Figure 5-1. You can create a sandbox database for free.

Figure 5-1. mLab

Adding Database to Context

Now it's time to connect to our database and add the connection to context. We are going to use a package called mongodb to communicate with our database. We can install this by using the command: npm install mongodb.

After we install this package, we will modify the Apollo Server configuration file, the index.js. We need to wait until mongodb successfully connects to our database to start the service. We also will need to pull the database host information from an environment variable called DB_HOST. We'll make this environment variable accessible in our project in a file called .env at the root of the project.

If you're using Mongo locally, your URL will look something like this:

```
DB_HOST=mongodb://localhost:27017/<Your-Database-Name>
```

If you're using mLab, your URL will look like this. Be sure to create a user and password for the database and replace <dbuser> and <dbpassword> with those values.

```
DB_HOST=mongodb://<dbuser>:<dbpassword>@5555.mlab.com:5555/<Your-Database-Name>
```

Let's connect to the database and build a context object before starting the service. We'll also use the dotenv package to load the DB_HOST URL:

```
const { MongoClient } = require('mongodb')
require('dotenv').config()

...

// 1. Create Asynchronous Function
async function start() {
  const app = express()
  const MONGO_DB = process.env.DB_HOST

  const client = await MongoClient.connect(
    MONGO_DB,
    { useNewUrlParser: true }
  )
  const db = client.db()

  const context = { db }

  const server = new ApolloServer({ typeDefs, resolvers, context })

  server.applyMiddleware({ app })

  app.get('/', (req, res) => res.end('Welcome to the PhotoShare API'))

  app.get('/playground', expressPlayground({ endpoint: '/graphql' }))

  app.listen({ port: 4000 }, () =>
    console.log(
      `GraphQL Server running at http://localhost:4000${server.graphqlPath}`
    )
  )
}

// 5. Invoke start when ready to start
start()
```

With start, we connect to the database. Connecting to a database is an asynchronous process. It will take some time to successfully connect to a database. This asynchronous function allows us to wait for a promise to resolve with the await keyword. The first thing we do in this function is wait for a successful connection to the local or remote database. After we have a database connection, we can add that connection to the context object and start our server.

Now we can modify our query resolvers to return information from our Mongo collections instead of local arrays. We'll also add queries for totalUsers and allUsers and add them to the schema:

Schema

```
type Query {
    ...
    totalUsers: Int!
    allUsers: [User!]!
}
```

Resolvers

```
Query: {

  totalPhotos: (parent, args, { db }) =>
      db.collection('photos')
        .estimatedDocumentCount(),

  allPhotos: (parent, args, { db }) =>
    db.collection('photos')
      .find()
      .toArray(),

  totalUsers: (parent, args, { db }) =>
    db.collection('users')
      .estimatedDocumentCount(),

  allUsers: (parent, args, { db }) =>
    db.collection('users')
      .find()
      .toArray()

}
```

`db.collection('photos')` is how you access a Mongo collection. We can count the documents in the collection with `.estimatedDocumentCount()`. We can list all of the documents in a collection and convert them to an array with `.find().toArray()`. At this point, the `photos` collection is empty, but this code will work. The `totalPhotos` and `totalUsers` resolver should return nothing. The `allPhotos` and `allUsers` resolvers should return empty arrays.

To add photos to the database, a user must be logged in. In the next section, we handle authorizing a user with GitHub and posting our first photo to the database.

GitHub Authorization

Authorizing and authenticating users is an important part of any application. There are a number of strategies that we can use to make this happen. Social authorization is a popular one because it leaves a lot of the account management details up to the social provider. It also can help users feel more secure when logging in, because the social provider might be a service with which they're already comfortable. For our application, we implement a GitHub authorization because it's highly likely that you already have a GitHub account (and if you don't, it's simple and quick to get one!).[1]

Setting Up GitHub OAuth

Before we get started, you need to set up GitHub authorization for this app to work. To do this, perform the following steps:

1. Go to *https://www.github.com* and log in.
2. Go to Account Settings.
3. Go to Developer Settings.
4. Click New OAuth App.
5. Add the following settings (as shown in Figure 5-2):

   Application name
       Localhost 3000

   Homepage URL
       http://localhost:3000

   Application description
       All authorizations for local GitHub Testing

   Authorization callback URL
       http://localhost:3000

---

1 You can create an account at *https://www.github.com*.

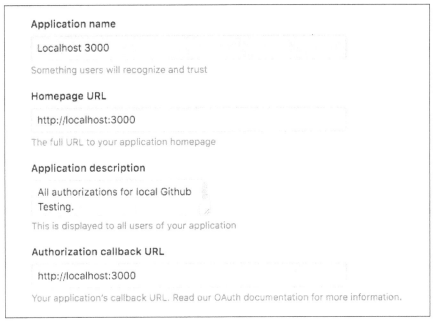

Figure 5-2. New OAuth App

6. Click Save.

7. Go to the OAuth Account Page and get your `client_id` and `client_secret`, as shown in Figure 5-3.

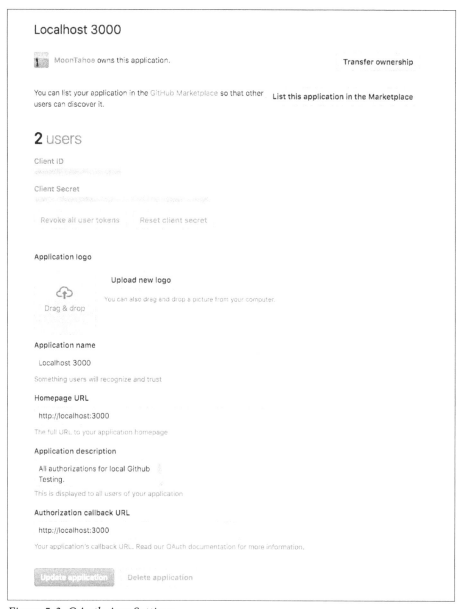

Figure 5-3. OAuth App Settings

With this setup in place, we can now get an `auth` token and information about the user from GitHub. Specifically, we will need the `client_id` and `client_secret`.

The Authorization Process

The process of authorizing a GitHub app happens on the client and the server. In this section, we discuss how to handle the server, and in Chapter 6, we go over the client implementation. As Figure 5-4 illustrates below, the full authorization process occurs in the following steps. Bold steps indicate what will happen in this chapter on the server:

1. Client: Asks GitHub for a code using a url with a `client_id`
2. User: Allows access to account information on GitHub for client application
3. GitHub: Sends code to OAuth redirect url: `http://localhost:3000?code=XYZ`
4. **Client: Sends GraphQL Mutation `githubAuth(code)` with code**
5. **API: Requests a GitHub `access_token` with credentials: `client_id`, `client_secret`, and `client_code`**
6. **GitHub: Responds with `access_token` that can be used with future info requests**
7. **API: Request user info with `access_token`**
8. **GitHub: Responds with user info: `name`, `githubLogin`, and `avatar`**
9. **API: Resolves `authUser(code)` mutation with `AuthPayload`, which contains a token and the user**
10. Client: Saves token to send with future GraphQL requests

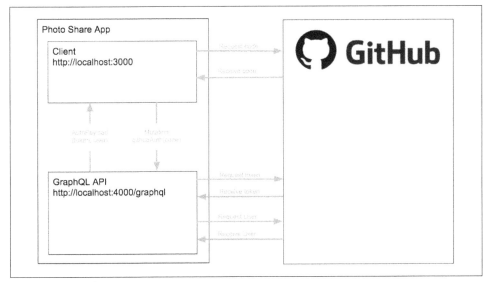

Figure 5-4. Authorization Process

To implement the `githubAuth` mutation, we'll assume that we have a code. After we use the code to obtain a token, we'll save the new user information and the token to our local database. We'll also return that info to the client. The client will save the token locally and send it back to us with each request. We'll use the token to authorize the user and access their data record.

githubAuth Mutation

We handle authorizing users by using a GitHub mutation. In Chapter 4, we designed a custom payload type for our schema called `AuthPayload`. Let's add the `AuthPayload` and the `githubAuth` mutation to our `typeDefs`:

```
type AuthPayload {
  token: String!
  user: User!
}

type Mutation {
  ...
  githubAuth(code: String!): AuthPayload!
}
```

The `AuthPayload` type is used only as a response to authorization mutations. It contains the user who was authorized by the mutation along with a token that they can use to identify themselves during future requests.

Before we program the `githubAuth` resolver, we need to build two functions to handle GitHub API requests:

```
const requestGithubToken = credentials =>
    fetch(
        'https://github.com/login/oauth/access_token',
        {
            method: 'POST',
            headers: {
                'Content-Type': 'application/json',
                Accept: 'application/json'
            },
            body: JSON.stringify(credentials)
        }
    )
    .then(res => res.json())
    .catch(error => {
      throw new Error(JSON.stringify(error))
    })
```

The `requestGithubToken` function returns a fetch promise. The `credentials` are sent to a GitHub API URL in the body of a POST request. The `credentials` consist of three things: the `client_id`, `client_secret`, and `code`. After it is completed, the GitHub response is then parsed as JSON. We can now use this function to request a

GitHub access token with `credentials`. This and future helper functions can be found in a `lib.js` file in the repo (*https://github.com/MoonHighway/learning-graphql/blob/master/chapter-05/photo-share-api/lib.js/*).

As soon as we have a GitHub token, we need to access information from the current user's account. Specifically, we want their GitHub login, name, and profile picture. To obtain this information, we need to send another request to the GitHub API along with the access `token` that we obtained from the previous request:

```
const requestGithubUserAccount = token =>
    fetch(`https://api.github.com/user?access_token=${token}`)
        .then(toJSON)
        .catch(throwError)
```

This function also returns a fetch promise. On this GitHub API route, we can access information about the current user so long as we have an access token.

Now, let's combine both of these requests into a single asynchronous function that we can use to authorize a user with GitHub:

```
async authorizeWithGithub(credentials) {
  const { access_token } = await requestGithubToken(credentials)
  const githubUser = await requestGithubUserAccount(access_token)
  return { ...githubUser, access_token }
}
```

Using `async`/`await` here makes it possible to handle multiple asynchronous requests. First, we request the access token and wait for the response. Then, using the `access_token`, we request the GitHub user account information and wait for a response. After we have the data, we'll put it all together in a single object.

We've created the helper functions that will support the functionality of the resolver. Now, let's actually write the resolver to obtain a token and a user account from GitHub:

```
async githubAuth(parent, { code }, { db }) {
  // 1. Obtain data from GitHub
    let {
      message,
      access_token,
      avatar_url,
      login,
      name
    } = await authorizeWithGithub({
      client_id: <YOUR_CLIENT_ID_HERE>,
      client_secret: <YOUR_CLIENT_SECRET_HERE>,
      code
    })
  // 2. If there is a message, something went wrong
    if (message) {
      throw new Error(message)
```

```
  }
// 3. Package the results into a single object
  let latestUserInfo = {
    name,
    githubLogin: login,
    githubToken: access_token,
    avatar: avatar_url
  }
// 4. Add or update the record with the new information
  const { ops:[user] } = await db
    .collection('users')
    .replaceOne({ githubLogin: login }, latestUserInfo, { upsert: true })
// 5. Return user data and their token
  return { user, token: access_token }

}
```

Resolvers can be asynchronous. We can wait for a network response before returning the result of an operation to a client. The githubAuth resolver is asynchronous because we must wait for two responses from GitHub before we'll have the data that we need to return.

After we have obtained the user's data from GitHub, we check our local database to see if this user has signed in to our app in the past, which would mean that they already have an account. If the user has an account, we will update their account details with the information that we received from GitHub. They might have changed their name or profile picture since they last logged in. If they do not already have an account, we will add the new user to our collection of users. In both cases, we return the logged in user and the token from this resolver.

It's time to test this authorization process, and to test, you need code. To obtain the code, you'll need to add your client ID to this URL:

```
https://github.com/login/oauth/authorize?client_id=YOUR-ID-HERE&scope=user
```

Paste the URL with your GitHub client_id into the location bar of a new browser window. You will be directed to GitHub, where you will agree to authorize this app. When you authorize the app, GitHub will redirect you back to http://localhost: 3000 with a code:

```
http://locahost:3000?code=XYZ
```

Here, the code is XYZ. Copy the code from the browser URL and then send it with the githubAuth mutation:

```
mutation {
  githubAuth(code:"XYZ") {
    token
    user {
      githubLogin
      name
```

```
      avatar
    }
  }
}
```

This mutation will authorize the current user and return a token along with information about that user. Save the token. We'll need to send it in the header with future requests.

Bad Credentials

When you see the error "Bad Credentials," the client ID, client secret, or code that was sent to the GitHub API is incorrect. Check the client ID and client secret to be sure; often it's the code that causes this error.

GitHub codes are good for only a limited time period and can be used only once. If there is a bug in the resolver after the credentials were requested, the code used in the request will no longer be valid. Typically, you can resolve this error by requesting another code from GitHub.

Authenticating Users

To identify yourself in future requests, you will need to send your token with every request in the Authorization header. That token will be used to identify the user by looking up their database record.

The GraphQL Playground has a location where you can add headers to each request. In the bottom corner, there is a tab right next to "Query Variables" called "HTTP Headers." You can add HTTP Headers to your request using this tab. Just send the headers as JSON:

```
{
  "Authorization": "<YOUR_TOKEN>"
}
```

Replace <YOUR_TOKEN> with the token that was returned from the githubAuth mutation. Now, you are sending the key to your identification with each GraphQL request. We need to use that key to find your account and add it to context.

me Query

From here, we want to create a query that refers back to our own user information: the me query. This query returns the current logged-in user based on the token sent in the HTTP headers of the request. If there is not currently a logged-in user, the query will return null.

The process begins when a client sends the GraphQL query, me, with `Authorization: token` for secure user information. The API then captures an `Authorization` header and uses the token to look up the current user record in the database. It also adds the current user account to context. After it's in context, every resolver will have access to the current user.

It's up to us to identify the current user and put them in context. Let's modify the configuration of our server. We'll need to change the way we build the context object. Instead of an object, we will use a function to handle context:

```
async function start() {
    const app = express()
    const MONGO_DB = process.env.DB_HOST

    const client = await MongoClient.connect(
      MONGO_DB,
      { useNewUrlParser: true }
    )

    const db = client.db()

    const server = new ApolloServer({
      typeDefs,
      resolvers,
      context: async ({ req }) => {
        const githubToken = req.headers.authorization
        const currentUser = await db.collection('users').findOne({ githubToken })
        return { db, currentUser }
      }
    })

    ...

}
```

Context can be an object or a function. For our application to work, we need it to be a function so that we can set the context every time there is a request. When context is a function, it is invoked for every GraphQL request. The object that is returned by this function is the context that is sent to the resolver.

In the context function, we can capture the authorization header from the request and parse it for the token. After we have a token, we can use it to look up a user in our database. If we have a user, they will be added to context. If not, the value for user in context will be null.

With this code in place, it is time to add the me query. First, we need to modify our `typeDefs`:

```
type Query {
  me: User
```

```
    ...
}
```

The me query returns a nullable user. It will be null if a current authorized user is not found. Let's add the resolver for the me query:

```
const resolvers = {
  Query: {
    me: (parent, args, { currentUser }) => currentUser,
    ...
  }
}
```

We've already done the heavy lifting of looking up the user based on their token. At this point, you'll simply return the currentUser object from context. Again, this will be null if there is not a user.

If the correct token has been added to the HTTP authorization header, you can send a request to obtain details about yourself using the me query:

```
query currentUser {
  me {
    githubLogin
    name
    avatar
  }
}
```

When you run this query, you will be identified. A good test to confirm that everything is correct is to try to run this query without the authorization header or with an incorrect token. Given a wrong token or missing header, you should see that the me query is null.

postPhoto mutation

To post a photo to our application, a user must be logged in. The postPhoto mutation can determine who is logged in by checking context. Let's modify the postPhoto mutation:

```
async postPhoto(parent, args, { db, currentUser }) {

    // 1. If there is not a user in context, throw an error
    if (!currentUser) {
        throw new Error('only an authorized user can post a photo')
    }

    // 2. Save the current user's id with the photo
    const newPhoto = {
        ...args.input,
        userID: currentUser.githubLogin,
        created: new Date()
    }
```

```
// 3. Insert the new photo, capture the id that the database created
const { insertedIds } = await db.collection('photos').insert(newPhoto)
newPhoto.id = insertedIds[0]

return newPhoto

}
```

The postPhoto mutation has undergone several changes in order to save a new photo to the database. First, the currentUser is obtained from context. If this value is null, we throw an error and prevent the postPhoto mutation from executing any further. To post a photo, the user must send the correct token in the Authorization header.

Next, we add the current user's ID to the newPhoto object. Now, we can save the new photo record to the photos collection in the database. Mongo creates a unique identifier for each document that it saves. When the new photo is added, we can obtain that identifier by using the insertedIds array. Before we return the photo, we need to make sure that it has a unique identifier.

We also need to change the Photo resolvers:

```
const resolvers = {
  ...
  Photo: {
    id: parent => parent.id || parent._id,
    url: parent => `/img/photos/${parent._id}.jpg`,
    postedBy: (parent, args, { db }) =>
      db.collection('users').findOne({ githubLogin: parent.userID })
}
```

First, if the client asks for a photo ID, we need to make sure it receives the correct value. If the parent photo does not already have an ID, we can assume that a database record has been created for the parent photo and it will have an ID saved under the field _id. We need to make sure that the ID field of the photo resolves to the database ID.

Next, let's assume that we are serving these photos from the same web server. We return the local route to the photo. This local route is created using the photo's ID.

Finally, we need to modify the postedBy resolver to look up the user who posted the photo in the database. We can use the userID that is saved with the parent photo to look up that user's record in the database. The photo's userID should match the users githubLogin, so the .findOne() method should return one user record, the user who posted the photo.

With our authorization header in place, we should be able to post new photos to the GraphQL service:

```
mutation post($input: PostPhotoInput!) {
  postPhoto(input: $input) {
    id
    url
    postedBy {
      name
      avatar
    }
  }
}
```

After we post the photo, we can ask for its `id` and `url`, along with the `name` and the `avatar` of the user who posted the photo.

Add fake users mutation

To test our application with users other than ourselves, we are going to add a muta-tion that will allow us to populate the database with fake users from the `random.me` API.

We can handle this with a mutation called `addFakeUsers`. Let's first add this to the schema:

```
type Mutation {
  addFakeUsers(count: Int = 1): [User!]!
  ...
}
```

Notice that the count argument takes in the number of fake users to add and returns a list of users. This list of users contains the accounts of the fake users added by this mutation. By default, we add one user at a time, but you can add more by sending this mutation a different count:

```
addFakeUsers: async (root, {count}, {db}) => {

    var randomUserApi = `https://randomuser.me/api/?results=${count}`

    var { results } = await fetch(randomUserApi)
      .then(res => res.json())

    var users = results.map(r => ({
      githubLogin: r.login.username,
      name: `${r.name.first} ${r.name.last}`,
      avatar: r.picture.thumbnail,
      githubToken: r.login.sha1
    }))

    await db.collection('users').insert(users)

    return users
}
```

To test adding new users, first we want to obtain some fake data from randomuser.me. addFakeUsers is an asynchronous function that we can use to fetch that data. Then, we serialize the data from randomuser.me, creating user objects that match our schema. Next, we add these new users to the database and return the list of new users.

Now, we can populate the database with a mutation:

```
mutation {
  addFakeUsers(count: 3) {
    name
  }
}
```

This mutation adds three fake users to the database. Now that we have fake users, we also want to sign in with a fake user account via a mutation. Let's add a fakeUserAuth to our Mutation type:

```
type Mutation {
  fakeUserAuth(githubLogin: ID!): AuthPayload!
  ...
}
```

Next, we need to add a resolver that returns a token that we can use to authorize our fake users:

```
async fakeUserAuth (parent, { githubLogin }, { db }) {

    var user = await db.collection('users').findOne({ githubLogin })

    if (!user) {
        throw new Error(`Cannot find user with githubLogin "${githubLogin}"`)
    }

    return {
        token: user.githubToken,
        user
    }

}
```

The fakeUserAuth resolver obtains the githubLogin from the mutation's arguments and uses it to find that user in the database. After it finds that user, the user's token and user account are returned in the shape of our AuthPayload type.

Now we can authenticate fake users by sending a mutation:

```
mutation {
  fakeUserAuth(githubLogin:"jDoe") {
    token
  }
}
```

Add the returned token to the authorization HTTP header to post new photos as this fake user.

Conclusion

Well, you did it. You built a GraphQL Server. You started by getting a thorough understanding of resolvers. You handled queries and mutations. You added GitHub authorization. You identified the current user via an access token that is added to the header of every request. And finally, you modified the mutation that reads the user from the resolver's context and allows users to post photos.

If you want to run a completed version of the service that we constructed in this chapter, you can find it in this book's repository (*https://github.com/MoonHighway/learning-graphql/tree/master/chapter-05/photo-share-api/*). This app will need to know what database to use and which GitHub OAuth credentials to use. You can add these values by created a new file named .env and placing it in the project root:

```
DB_HOST=<YOUR_MONGODB_HOST>
CLIENT_ID=<YOUR_GITHUB_CLIENT_ID>
CLIENT_SECRET=<YOUR_GITHUB_CLIENT_SECRET>
```

With the .env file in place, you are ready to install the dependencies: yarn or npm install and run the service: yarn start or npm start. Once the service is running on port 4000, you can send queries to it using the Playground at: http://localhost:4000/playground. You can request a GitHub code by clicking the link found at http://localhost:4000. If you want to access the GraphQL endpoint from some other client, you can find it at: http://localhost:4000/graphql.

In Chapter 7, we show you how to modify this API to handle subscriptions and file uploads. But before we do that, we need to show you how clients will consume this API, so in Chapter 6, we look at how to construct a frontend that can work with this service.

GraphQL Clients

With your GraphQL server built, it's now time to set up GraphQL on the client side. Very broadly, a client is just an application that communicates with a server. Because of the flexibility of GraphQL, there's no prescription for how to build a client. You might be building apps for web browsers. You might be creating native applications for phones. You might be building a GraphQL service for a screen on your refrigerator. It also does not matter to the client in which language the service is written.

All you really need to send queries and mutations is the ability to send an HTTP request. When the service responds with some data, you can use it in your client no matter what that client is.

Using a GraphQL API

The easiest way to begin is just to make an HTTP request to your GraphQL endpoint. To test the server that we built in Chapter 5, make sure your service is running locally at *http://localhost:4000/graphql*. You can also find all of these samples running on CodeSandbox at the links found in the Chapter 6 repository (*https://github.com/Moon Highway/learning-graphql/tree/master/chapter-06*).

fetch Requests

As you saw in Chapter 3, you can send requests to a GraphQL service by using cURL. All you need is a few different values:

- A query: `{totalPhotos, totalUsers}`
- A GraphQL endpoint: `http://localhost:4000/graphql`
- A content type: `Content-Type: application/json`

From there, you send the cURL request directly from the terminal/command prompt using the POST method:

```
curl -X POST \
    -H "Content-Type: application/json" \
    --data '{ "query": "{totalUsers, totalPhotos}" }' \
    http://localhost:4000/graphql
```

If we send this request, we should see the correct results, {"data":{"totalUsers": 7,"totalPhotos":4}}, as JSON data returned in the terminal. Your numbers for totalUsers and totalPhotos will reflect your current data. If your client is a shell script, you can start building that script with cURL.

Because we're using cURL, we can use anything that sends an HTTP request. We could build a tiny client by using fetch, which will work in the browser:

```
var query = `{totalPhotos, totalUsers}`
var url = 'http://localhost:4000/graphql'

var opts = {
  method: 'POST',
  headers: { 'Content-Type': 'application/json' },
  body: JSON.stringify({ query })
}

fetch(url, opts)
  .then(res => res.json())
  .then(console.log)
  .catch(console.error)
```

After we fetch the data, we'll see the expected result logged in the console:

```
{
  "data": {
    "totalPhotos": 4,
    "totalUsers": 7
  }
}
```

We can use the resulting data on the client to build applications. Let's consider a basic example to see how we might list totalUsers and totalPhotos directly in the DOM:

```
fetch(url, opts)
  .then(res => res.json())
  .then(({data}) => `
      <p>photos: ${data.totalPhotos}</p>
      <p>users: ${data.totalUsers}</p>
  `)
  .then(text => document.body.innerHTML = text)
  .catch(console.error)
```

Instead of logging the results to the console, we use the data to build some HTML text. We can then take that text and write it directly to the document's body. Be careful: it's possible to overwrite anything that was in the body after the request is complete.

If you already know how to send HTTP requests using your favorite client, you already have the tools necessary to build a client application that communicates with any GraphQL API.

graphql-request

Though cURL and fetch work well, there are other frameworks that you can use to send GraphQL operations to an API. One of the most notable examples of this is graphql-request. graphql-request wraps fetch requests in a promise that can be used to make requests to the GraphQL server. It also handles the details of making the request and parsing the data for you.

To get started with graphql-request, you first need to install it:

```
npm install graphql-request
```

From there, you import and use the module as request. Be sure to keep the photo service running on port 4000:

```
import { request } from 'graphql-request'

var query = `
  query listUsers {
    allUsers {
      name
      avatar
    }
  }
`

request('http://localhost:4000/graphql', query)
    .then(console.log)
    .catch(console.error)
```

The request function takes in url and query, makes the request to the server, and returns the data in one line of code. The data returned is, as expected, a JSON response of all of the users:

```
{
  "allUsers": [
    { "name": "sharon adams", "avatar": "http://..." },
    { "name": "sarah ronau", "avatar": "http://..." },
    { "name": "paul young", "avatar": "http://..." },
  ]
}
```

We can begin using this data in our client straight away.

You can also send mutations with `graphql-request`:

```
import { request } from 'graphql-request'

var url = 'http://localhost:4000/graphql'

var mutation = `
    mutation populate($count: Int!) {
        addFakeUsers(count:$count) {
            id
            name
        }
    }
`

var variables = { count: 3 }

request(url, mutation, variables)
    .then(console.log)
    .catch(console.error)
```

The `request` function takes in the API URL, the mutation, and a third argument for variables. This is just a JavaScript object that passes in a field and value for the query variables. After we invoke `request`, we issue the `addFakeUsers` mutation.

Though `graphql-request` doesn't offer any formal integration with UI libraries and frameworks, we can incorporate a library fairly simply. Let's load some data into a React component using `graphql-request`, as demonstrated in Example 6-1.

Example 6-1. GraphQL Request and React

```
import React from 'react'
import ReactDOM from 'react-dom'
import { request } from 'graphql-request'

var url = 'http://localhost:4000/graphql'

var query = `
  query listUsers {
    allUsers {
      avatar
      name
    }
  }
`

var mutation = `
    mutation populate($count: Int!) {
        addFakeUsers(count:$count) {
            githubLogin
        }
```

```
    }

const App = ({ users=[] }) =>
    <div>
        {users.map(user =>
            <div key={user.githubLogin}>
                <img src={user.avatar} alt="" />
                {user.name}
            </div>
        )}
        <button onClick={addUser}>Add User</button>
    </div>

const render = ({ allUsers=[] }) =>
    ReactDOM.render(
        <App users={allUsers} />,
        document.getElementById('root')
    )

const addUser = () =>
    request(url, mutation, {count:1})
        .then(requestAndRender)
        .catch(console.error)

const requestAndRender = () =>
    request(url, query)
        .then(render)
        .catch(console.error)

requestAndRender()
```

Our file starts with an import of both React and ReactDOM. We then create an App component. App maps over the users that are passed as props and creates div elements containing their avatar and username. The render function renders the App to the #root element and passes in allUsers as a property.

From there, requestAndRender calls request from graphql-request. This issues the query, receives the data, and then calls render, which provides the data to the App component.

This little app also handles mutations. In the App component, the button has an onClick event that calls the addUser function. When invoked, this sends the mutation and then calls requestAndRender to issue a new request for the services users and rerenders the <App /> with the new list of users.

So far, we've looked at a few different ways to begin building client apps using GraphQL. You can write shell scripts with cURL. You can build web pages with fetch. You can build apps a little faster with graphql-request. You could stop right there if you wanted to, but there are even more powerful GraphQL clients available. Let's go for it.

Apollo Client

A huge benefit of using Representational State Transfer (REST) is the ease with which you can handle caching. With REST, you can save the response data from a request in a cache under the URL that was used to access that request. Caching done, no problem. Caching GraphQL is a little trickier. We don't have a multitude of routes with a GraphQL API—everything is sent and received over a single endpoint, so we cannot simply save the data returned from a route under the URL that was used to request it.

To build a robust, performant application, we need a way to cache queries and their resulting objects. Having a localized caching solution is essential as we constantly strive to create fast, efficient apps. We could create something like this ourselves, or we could lean on one of the vetted clients that already exist.

The most prominent GraphQL client solutions available today are Relay and Apollo Client. Relay was open sourced by Facebook in 2015 at the same time as GraphQL. It brings together everything that Facebook learned about using GraphQL in production. Relay is compatible with React and React Native only, which means that there was an opportunity to create a GraphQL client to support developers who might not use React.

Enter Apollo Client. Brought to you by Meteor Development Group, Apollo Client is a community-driven project to build a flexible GraphQL client solution to handle tasks like caching, optimistic UI updates, and more. The team has created packages that supply bindings for React, Angular, Ember, Vue, iOS, and Android.

We've already been using several tools from the Apollo team on the server, but Apollo Client focuses specifically on sending and receiving requests from the client to the server. It handles the network requests with Apollo Link and handles all caching with Apollo Cache. Apollo Client then wraps the link and the cache and manages all interactions with the GraphQL service efficiently.

For the rest of the chapter, we take a closer look at Apollo Client. We're going to be using React to build out our UI components, but we can apply many of the techniques described here to projects that use different libraries and frameworks.

Apollo Client with React

Since working with React is what led us to GraphQL in the first place, we have chosen React as the user interface library. We haven't offered much explanation about React itself. It is a library that was created at Facebook that uses a component-based architecture to compose UIs. If you are a user of a different library and you never want to look at React again after this, that's ok. The ideas presented in this next section are applicable to other UI frameworks.

Project Setup

In this chapter, we show you how to build a React app that interacts with a GraphQL service using Apollo Client. To begin, we need to scaffold the frontend of this project using `create-react-app`. `create-react-app` allows you to generate an entire React project without setting up any build configuration. If you haven't used `create-react-app` before, you might need to install it:

```
npm install -g create-react-app
```

Once installed, you can create a React project anywhere on your computer with:

```
create-react-app photo-share-client
```

This command installs a new base React application in a folder named *photo-share-client*. It automatically adds and installs everything that you will need to get started building a React app. To start the application, navigate to the *photo-share-client* folder and run `npm start`. You'll see your browser open to `http://localhost:3000` where your React client application is running. Remember, you can find all of the files for this chapter in the repository at *http://github.com/moonhighway/learning-graphql*.

Configure Apollo Client

You'll need to install a few packages to build a GraphQL client with Apollo tools. First, you'll need `graphql` which includes the GraphQL language parser. Then you'll need a package called `apollo-boost`. Apollo Boost includes the Apollo packages necessary for creating an Apollo Client and sending operations to that client. Finally, we'll need `react-apollo`. React Apollo is an npm library that contains React components that we will use to construct a user interface with Apollo.

Let's install these three packages at the same time:

```
npm install graphql apollo-boost react-apollo
```

Now we are ready to create our client. The `ApolloClient` constructor found in `apollo-boost` can be used to create our first client. Open the *src/index.js* file and replace the code in that file with the following:

```
import ApolloClient from 'apollo-boost'

const client = new ApolloClient({ uri: 'http://localhost:4000/graphql' })
```

Using the `ApolloClient` constructor, we've created a new `client` instance. The `client` is ready to handle all network communication with the GraphQL service hosted at `http://localhost:4000/graphql`. For example, we can use the client to send a query to the PhotoShare Service:

```
import ApolloClient, { gql } from 'apollo-boost'

const client = new ApolloClient({ uri: 'http://localhost:4000/graphql' })

const query = gql`
    {
        totalUsers
        totalPhotos
    }
    `

client.query({query})
    .then(({ data }) => console.log('data', data))
    .catch(console.error)
```

This code uses the `client` to send a query for the total photo count and the total user count. To make this happen, we imported the `gql` function from `apollo-boost`. This function is a part of the `graphql-tag` package that was automatically included with `apollo-boost`. The `gql` function is used to parse a query into an AST or abstract syntax tree.

We can send the AST to the client by invoking `client.query({query})`. This method returns a promise. It sends the query as an HTTP request to our GraphQL service and resolves the data returned from that service. In the above example, we are logging the response to the console:

```
{ totalUsers: 4, totalPhotos: 7, Symbol(id): "ROOT_QUERY" }
```

 GraphQL Service Should Be Running

Make sure that the GraphQL service is still running on `http://localhost:4000` so that you can test the client connection to the server.

In addition to handling all network requests to our GraphQL service, the client also caches the responses locally in memory. At any point, we can take a look at the cache by invoking `client.extract()`:

```
console.log('cache', client.extract())
client.query({query})
    .then(() => console.log('cache', client.extract()))
    .catch(console.error)
```

Here we have a look at the cache before the query is sent, and another look at it after the query has been resolved. We can see that we now have the results saved in a local object which is managed by the client:

```
{
    ROOT_QUERY: {
        totalPhotos: 4,
        totalUsers: 7
    }
}
```

The next time we send the client a query for this data, it will read it from the cache as opposed to sending another network request to our service. Apollo Client provides us with options to specify when, and how often, we should send HTTP requests over the network. We'll cover those options later on in this chapter. For now, it is important to understand that Apollo Client is used to handle all network requests to our GraphQL service. Additionally, by default, it automatically caches the results locally and defers to the local cache to improve our applications performance.

To get started with react-apollo, all we need to do is create a client and add it to our user interface with a component called ApolloProvider. Replace the code found in the index.js file with the following:

```
import React from 'react'
import { render } from 'react-dom'
import App from './App'
import { ApolloProvider } from 'react-apollo'
import ApolloClient from 'apollo-boost'

const client = new ApolloClient({ uri: 'http://localhost:4000/graphql' })

render(
    <ApolloProvider client={client}>
      <App />
    </ApolloProvider>,
    document.getElementById('root')
)
```

This is all the code you will need to get started using Apollo with React. Here, we've created a client and then placed that client in React's global scope with the help of a component called the ApolloProvider. Any child component wrapped by the Apollo Provider will have access to the client. That means that the <App /> component and any of its children are ready to receive data from our GraphQL service via Apollo Client.

The Query Component

Using Apollo Client, we need a way to handle queries to fetch data to load into our React UI. The Query component will take care of fetching data, handling loading state, and updating our UI. We can use the Query component anywhere within the ApolloProvider. The Query component sends a query using the client. Once resolved, the client will return the results that we'll use to construct the user interface.

Open the src/App.js file and replace the code that is currently inside of this file with the following:

```
import React from 'react'
import Users from './Users'
import { gql } from 'apollo-boost'

export const ROOT_QUERY = gql`
    query allUsers {
        totalUsers
        allUsers {
            githubLogin
            name
            avatar
        }
    }
`


const App = () => <Users />

export default App
```

In the App component, we've created a query called ROOT_QUERY. Remember, one of the benefits of using GraphQL is to request everything you'll need to construct your UI and receive all of that data in a single response. That means we are going to request both the totalUsers count and the allUsers array in a query that we've created in the root of our application. Using the gql function, we've converted our string query an AST object named ROOT_QUERY, and we've exported this object so that other components can use it.

At this point, you should see an error. This is because we've told the App to render a component that we have not created. Create a new file called src/Users.js and place this code inside of that file:

```
import React from 'react'
import { Query } from 'react-apollo'
import { ROOT_QUERY } from './App'

const Users = () =>
    <Query query={ROOT_QUERY}>
        {result =>
            <p>Users are loading: {result.loading ? "yes" : "no"}</p>
        }
    </Query>

export default Users
```

Now you should see the error clear, and the message "Users are loading: no" should be displayed in the browser window. Under the hood, the Query component is sending the ROOT_QUERY to our GraphQL service and caching the result locally. We obtain the result using a React technique called render props. Render props allow us to pass properties as function arguments to child components. Notice that we are obtaining the result from a function and returning a paragraph element.

The result contains more information than just the response data. It will tell us whether or not an operation is loading via the result.loading property. In the preceding example, we can tell the user whether or not the current query is loading.

Throttle the HTTP Request

Your network might be too fast to see more than a quick flicker of the loading property in the browser. You can use the Network tab in Chrome's developer tools to throttle the HTTP request. In the developer tools, you'll find a dropdown that has the "Online" option selected. Selecting "Slow 3G" from the dropdown will simulate a slower response. This will allow you to see the loading happen in the browser.

Once the data has loaded, it will be passed along with the result.

Instead of displaying "yes" or "no" when the client is loading data, we can display UI components instead. Let's adjust the Users.js file:

```
const Users = () =>
    <Query query={ROOT_QUERY}>
        {({ data, loading }) => loading ?
            <p>loading users...</p> :
            <UserList count={data.totalUsers} users={data.allUsers} />
        }
    </Query>


const UserList = ({ count, users }) =>
    <div>
        <p>{count} Users</p>
        <ul>
            {users.map(user =>
                <UserListItem key={user.githubLogin}
                    name={user.name}
                    avatar={user.avatar} />
            )}
        </ul>
    </div>

const UserListItem = ({ name, avatar }) =>
    <li>
        <img src={avatar} width={48} height={48} alt="" />
        {name}
    </li>
```

If the client is loading the current query, we will display a "loading users..." message. If the data has been loaded, we will pass the total user count along with an array containing the name, githubLogin, and avatar of every user to the UserList component: exactly the data we asked for in our query. The UserList uses the result data to build the UI. It displays the count along with a list that displays the user's avatar image alongside of their name.

The results object also has several utility functions for pagination, refetching, and polling. Let's use the refetch function to refetch the list of users when we click a button:

```
const Users = () =>
    <Query query={ROOT_QUERY}>
        {(({ data, loading, refetch }) => loading ?
            <p>loading users...</p> :
            <UserList count={data.totalUsers}
                users={data.allUsers}
                refetchUsers={refetch} />
        }
    </Query>
```

Here we've obtained a function that can be used to refetch the ROOT_QUERY or request the data from the server again. The refetch property is simply a function. We can pass it to the UserList where it can be added to a button click:

```
const UserList = ({ count, users, refetch }) =>
    <div>
        <p>{count} Users</p>
        <button onClick={() => refetch()}>Refetch</button>
        <ul>
            {users.map(user =>
                <UserListItem key={user.githubLogin}
                    name={user.name}
                    avatar={user.avatar} />
            )}
        </ul>
    </div>
```

In the UserList, we are using the refetch function to request the same root data from our GraphQL service. Whenever you click the "Refetch Users" button, another query will be sent to the GraphQL endpoint to refetch any data changes. This is one way to keep your user interface in sync with the data on the server.

 To test this, we can change the user data after the initial fetch. You can delete the users collection, delete user documents directly from MongoDB, or add fake users by sending a query with the server's GraphQL Playground. When you change the data in the database, the "Refetch Users" button will need to be clicked in order to re-render the most up to date data in the browser.

Polling is another option that is available with the `Query` component. When we add the `pollInterval` prop to the `Query` component, data is automatically fetched over and over again based on a given interval:

```
<Query query={ROOT_QUERY} pollInterval={1000}>
```

Setting a `pollInterval` automatically refetches the data at a specified time. In this case, we will refetch the data from the server every second. Be careful when using polling as this code actually sends a new network request every second.

In addition to `loading`, `data`, and `refetch`, the response object has some additional options:

`stopPolling`
A function that stops polling

`startPolling`
A function that will start polling

`fetchMore`
A function that can be used to fetch the next page of data

Before we continue, remove any `pollInterval` properties from the `Query` component. We do not want polling to take place as we continue to iterate on this example.

The Mutation Component

When we want to send mutations to the GraphQL service, we can use the `Mutation` component. In the next example, we use this component to handle the `addFakeUsers` mutation. When we send this mutation, we write the new list of users directly to the cache.

To begin, let's import the `Mutation` component and add a mutation to the `Users.js` file:

```
import { Query, Mutation } from 'react-apollo'
import { gql } from 'apollo-boost'

...

const ADD_FAKE_USERS_MUTATION = gql`
    mutation addFakeUsers($count:Int!) {
        addFakeUsers(count:$count) {
            githubLogin
            name
            avatar
        }
    }
`
```

Once we have the mutation, we can use it in combination with the `Mutation` component. This component will pass a function to its children via render props. This function can be used to send the mutation when we are ready:

```
const UserList = ({ count, users, refetchUsers }) =>
    <div>
        <p>{count} Users</p>
        <button onClick={() => refetchUsers()}>Refetch Users</button>
        <Mutation mutation={ADD_FAKE_USERS_MUTATION} variables={{ count: 1 }}>
            {addFakeUsers =>
                <button onClick={addFakeUsers}>Add Fake Users</button>
            }
        </Mutation>
        <ul>
            {users.map(user =>
                <UserListItem key={user.githubLogin}
                    name={user.name}
                    avatar={user.avatar} />
            )}
        </ul>
    </div>
```

Just as we sent `query` as a prop to the `Query` component, we will send a `mutation` prop to the `Mutation` component. Notice also that we're using the `variables` property. This will send the necessary query variables with the mutation. In this case, it sets the count to 1, which will cause the mutation to add one fake user at a time. The `Mutation` component uses a function, `addFakeUsers`, that will send the mutation once it has been invoked. When the user clicks the "Add Fake Users" button, the mutation will be sent to our API.

Currently, these users are being added to the database, but the only way to see the changes is to click the "Refetch Users" button. We can tell the `Mutation` component to refetch specific queries once the mutation has completed instead of waiting for our users to click a button:

```
<Mutation mutation={ADD_FAKE_USERS_MUTATION}
    variables={{ count: 1 }}
    refetchQueries={[{ query: ROOT_QUERY }]}>
    {addFakeUsers =>
        <button onClick={addFakeUsers}>Add Fake Users</button>
    }
</Mutation>
```

`refetchQueries` is a property that lets you specify which queries to refetch after sending a mutation. Simply place a list of objects that contain queries. Each of the query operations found in this list will refetch data after the mutation has completed.

Authorization

In Chapter 5, we built a mutation to authorize a user with GitHub. In the following section, we show you how to set up user authorization on the client side.

The process of authorizing a user involves several steps. The bold steps indicate the functionality we'll add to the client:

Client
> Redirects the user to GitHub with the `client_id`

User
> Allows access to account information on GitHub for the client application

GitHub
> Redirects back to the website with code: `http://localhost:3000?code=XYZ`

Client
> Sends GraphQL Mutation `authUser(code)` with code

API
> Requests a GitHub `access_token` with `client_id`, `client_secret`, and `client_code`

GitHub
> Responds with `access_token` that can be used with future info requests

API
> Request user info with `access_token`

GitHub
> Responds with user info: `name`, `github_login`, `avatar_url`

API
> Resolves `authUser(code)` mutation with `AuthPayload`, which contains a token and the user

Client
> Saves token to send with future GraphQL requests

Authorizing the User

It is now time to authorize the user. To facilitate this example, we use React Router, which we install via npm: `npm install react-router-dom`.

Let's modify our main `<App />` component. We'll incorporate the `BrowserRouter`, and we'll add a new component, `AuthorizedUser`, that we can use to authorize users with GitHub:

```
import React from 'react'
import Users from './Users'
import { BrowserRouter } from 'react-router-dom'
import { gql } from 'apollo-boost'
import AuthorizedUser from './AuthorizedUser'

export const ROOT_QUERY = gql`
    query allUsers {
        totalUsers
        allUsers { ...userInfo }
        me { ...userInfo }
    }

    fragment userInfo on User {
        githubLogin
        name
        avatar
    }
`

const App = () =>
  <BrowserRouter>
    <div>
        <AuthorizedUser />
        <Users />
    </div>
  </BrowserRouter>

export default App
```

BrowserRouter wraps all of the other components that we want to render. We also will add a new AuthorizedUser component, which we will build in a new file. We should see an error until we add that component.

We've also modified the ROOT_QUERY to get it ready for authorization. We are now additionally asking for the me field, which returns information about the current user when someone is logged in. When a user is not logged in, this field will simply return null. Notice that we've added a fragment called userInfo to the query document. This allows us obtain the same information about a User in two places: the me field and the allUsers field.

The AuthorizedUser component should redirect the user to GitHub to request a code. That code should be passed back from GitHub to our app at http://local host:3000.

In a new file called AuthorizedUser.js, let's implement this process:

```
import React, { Component } from 'react'
import { withRouter } from 'react-router-dom'

class AuthorizedUser extends Component {
```

```
    state = { signingIn: false }

    componentDidMount() {
        if (window.location.search.match(/code=/)) {
            this.setState({ signingIn: true })
            const code = window.location.search.replace("?code=", "")
            alert(code)
            this.props.history.replace('/')
        }
    }

    requestCode() {
      var clientID = <YOUR_GITHUB_CLIENT_ID>
      window.location =
        `https://github.com/login/oauth/authorize?client_id=${clientID}&scope=user`
    }

    render() {
        return (
          <button onClick={this.requestCode} disabled={this.state.signingIn}>
              Sign In with GitHub
          </button>
        )
    }
}

export default withRouter(AuthorizedUser)
```

The AuthorizedUser component renders a "Sign In with GitHub" button. Once clicked, this button will redirect the user to GitHub's OAuth process. Once authorized, GitHub will pass a code back to the browser: http://localhost:3000?code=XYZGNARLYSENDABC. If the code is found in the query string, the component parses it from the window's location and displays it in an alert box to the user before removing it with the history property that was sent to this component with React Router.

Instead of sending the user an alert with the GitHub code, we need to send it to the githubAuth mutation:

```
import { Mutation } from 'react-apollo'
import { gql } from 'apollo-boost'
import { ROOT_QUERY } from './App'

const GITHUB_AUTH_MUTATION = gql`
    mutation githubAuth($code:String!) {
        githubAuth(code:$code) { token }
    }
`
```

The above mutation will be used to authorize the current user. All we need is the code. Let's add this mutation to the render method of this component:

```
render() {
    return (
        <Mutation mutation={GITHUB_AUTH_MUTATION}
            update={this.authorizationComplete}
            refetchQueries={[{ query: ROOT_QUERY }]}>

            {mutation => {
                this.githubAuthMutation = mutation
                return (
                    <button
                        onClick={this.requestCode}
                        disabled={this.state.signingIn}>
                        Sign In with GitHub
                    </button>
                )
            }}

        </Mutation>
    )
}
```

The Mutation component is tied to the GITHUB_AUTH_MUTATION. Once completed, it will invoke the component's authorizationComplete method and refetch the ROOT_QUERY. The mutation function has been added to the scope of the Authorize dUser component by setting: this.githubAuthMutation = mutation. We can now invoke this this.githubAuthMutation() function when we are ready (when we have a code).

Instead of alerting the code, we will send it along with the mutation to authorize the current user. Once authorized, we will save the resulting token to localStorage and use the router's history property to remove the code from the window's location:

```
class AuthorizedUser extends Component {

    state = { signingIn: false }

    authorizationComplete = (cache, { data }) => {
        localStorage.setItem('token', data.githubAuth.token)
        this.props.history.replace('/')
        this.setState({ signingIn: false })
    }

    componentDidMount() {
        if (window.location.search.match(/code=/)) {
            this.setState({ signingIn: true })
            const code = window.location.search.replace("?code=", "")
            this.githubAuthMutation({ variables: {code} })
        }
```

```
        }

        ...

    }
```

To start the authorization process, invoke `this.githubAuthMutation()` and add the code to the operation's `variables`. Once complete, the `authorizationComplete` method will be called. The `data` passed to this method is the data that we selected in the mutation. It has a `token`. We'll save the `token` locally and use React Router's `history` to remove the code query string from the window's location bar.

At this point, we will have signed in the current user with GitHub. The next step will be to make sure that we send this token along with every request in the HTTP headers.

Identifying the User

Our next task is to add a token to the authorization header for each request. Remember, the `photo-share-api` service that we created in the last chapter will identify users who pass an authorization token in the header. All we have to do is make sure any token saved to `localStorage` is sent along with every request sent to our GraphQL service.

Let's modify the `src/index.js` file. We need to find the line where we create the Apollo Client and replace it with this code:

```
const client = new ApolloClient({
    uri: 'http://localhost:4000/graphql',
    request: operation => {
        operation.setContext(context => ({
            headers: {
                ...context.headers,
                authorization: localStorage.getItem('token')
            }
        }))
    }
})
```

We've now added a request method to our Apollo Client configuration. This method passes the details about every `operation` just before it is sent to the GraphQL service. Here we are setting the context of every `operation` to include an `authorization` header that contains the token saved to local storage. Don't worry, if we don't have a token saved the value of this header will simply be null and our service will assume that there a user has not been authorized.

Now that we've added the authorization token to every header, our `me` field should return data about the current user. Let's display that data in our UI. Find the `render` method in the `AuthorizedUser` component and replace it with this code:

```
render() {
    return (
        <Mutation
            mutation={GITHUB_AUTH_MUTATION}
            update={this.authorizationComplete}
            refetchQueries={[[{ query: ROOT_QUERY }]]}>
            {mutation => {
                this.githubAuthMutation = mutation
                return (
                    <Me signingIn={this.state.signingIn}
                        requestCode={this.requestCode}
                        logout={() => localStorage.removeItem('token')} />
                )
            }}
        </Mutation>
    )
}
```

Instead of rendering a button, this `Mutation` component now renders a component called `Me`. The `Me` component will either display information about the current user who is logged in or the authorize button. It will need to know whether or not the user is currently in the process of signing in. It also needs to access the `requestCode` methods of the `AuthorizedUser` component. Finally, we need to provide a function that can log the current user out. For now, we'll just remove the `token` from `localStorage` when the user logs out. All of these values have been passed down to the `Me` component as properties.

It's now time to create the `Me` component. Add the following code above the declaration of the `AuthorizedUser` component:

```
const Me = ({ logout, requestCode, signingIn }) =>
    <Query query={ROOT_QUERY}>
        {({ loading, data }) => data.me ?
            <CurrentUser {...data.me} logout={logout} /> :
            loading ?
                <p>loading... </p> :
                <button
                    onClick={requestCode}
                    disabled={signingIn}>
                        Sign In with GitHub
                </button>
        }
    </Query>

const CurrentUser = ({ name, avatar, logout }) =>
    <div>
```

```
        <img src={avatar} width={48} height={48} alt="" />
        <h1>{name}</h1>
        <button onClick={logout}>logout</button>
    </div>
```

The Me component renders a Query component to obtain the data about the current user from the ROOT_QUERY. If there is a token, the me field in the ROOT_QUERY will not be null. Within the query component, we check to see if data.me is null. If there is data under this field, we will display the CurrentUser component and pass the data about the current user to this component as properties. The code {...data.me} uses the spread operator to pass all of the fields to the CurrentUser component as individual properties. Additionally, the logout function is passed to the CurrentUser component. When the user clicks the logout button, this function will be invoked and their token removed.

Working with the Cache

As developers, we're in the network request minimization business. We don't want our users to have to make extraneous requests. In order to minimize the number of network requests that our apps send, we can dig deeper into how to customize the Apollo Cache.

Fetch Policies

By default, Apollo Client stores data in a local JavaScript variable. Every time we create a client, a cache is created for us. Every time we send an operation, the response is cached locally. The fetchPolicy tells Apollo Client where to look for data to resolve an operation: either the local cache or a network request. The default fetchPolicy is cache-first. This means that the client will look locally in the cache for data to resolve the operation. If the client can resolve the operation without sending a network request, it will do so. However, if data to resolve the query is not in the cache then the client will send a network request to the GraphQL service.

Another type of fetchPolicy is cache-only. This policy tells the client to only look in the cache and never send a network request. If the data to fulfill the query does not exist in the cache, then an error will be thrown.

Take a look at src/Users.js, and find the Query inside the Users component. We can change the fetch policy of individual queries simply by adding the fetchPolicy property:

```
<Query query={{ query: ROOT_QUERY }} fetchPolicy="cache-only">
```

At present, if we set the policy for this Query to cache-only and refresh the browser, we should see an error because Apollo Client is only looking in the cache for the data to resolve our query and that data is not present when the app starts. To clear the error, change the fetch policy to `cache-and-network`:

```
<Query query={{ query: ROOT_QUERY }} fetchPolicy="cache-and-network">
```

The application works again. The `cache-and-network` policy always resolves the query immediately from the cache and additionally sends a network request to get the latest data. If the local cache does not exist, as is the case when the app starts, this policy will simply retrieve the data from the network. Other policies include:

`network-only`
:   Always sends a network request to resolve a query

`no-cache`
:   Always sends a network request to resolve the data and it doesn't cache the resulting response

Persisting The Cache

It is possible to save the cache locally on the client. This unlocks the power of the `cache-first` policy, because the cache will already exist when the user returns to the application. In this case, the `cache-first` policy will immediately resolve the data from the existing local cache and not send a request to the network at all.

To save cache data locally, we'll need to install an npm package:

```
npm install apollo-cache-persist
```

The `apollo-cache-persist` package contains a function that enhances the cache by saving it to a local store whenever it changes. To implement cache persistance, we'll need to create our own cache object and add it to the `client` when we configure our application.

Add the following code to the `src/index.js` file:

```
import ApolloClient, { InMemoryCache } from 'apollo-boost'
import { persistCache } from 'apollo-cache-persist'

const cache = new InMemoryCache()
persistCache({
    cache,
    storage: localStorage
})

const client = new ApolloClient({
    cache,

    ...

})
```

First, we've created our own cache instance using the `InMemoryCache` constructor provided with `apollo-boost`. Next, we imported the `persistCache` method from `apollo-cache-persist`. Using `InMemoryCache`, we create a new cache instance and send it to the `persistCache` method along with a `storage` location. We've chosen to save the cache in the browser window's `localStorage` store. This means that once we start our application, we should see the value of our cache saved to our store. You can check for it by adding the following syntax:

```
console.log(localStorage['apollo-cache-persist'])
```

The next step is to check `localStorage` on startup to see if we already have a cache saved. If we do, then we'll want to initialize our local `cache` with that data before creating the client:

```
const cache = new InMemoryCache()
persistCache({
    cache,
    storage: localStorage
})

if (localStorage['apollo-cache-persist']) {
    let cacheData = JSON.parse(localStorage['apollo-cache-persist'])
    cache.restore(cacheData)
}
```

Now our application will load any cached data before it starts. If we do have data saved under the key `apollo-cache-persist`, then we'll use the `cache.restore(cacheData)` method to add it to the `cache` instance.

We've successfully minimized the number of network requests to our service simply by using Apollo Client's cache effectively. In the next section, we will learn about how we can write data directly to the local cache.

Updating the Cache

The `Query` component is capable of reading directly from the cache. That's what makes a fetch policy like `cache-only` possible. We are also able to interact directly with the Apollo Cache. We can read current data from the cache or write data directly to the cache. Every time we change data stored in the cache, `react-apollo` detects that change and re-renders all of the effected components. All we have to do is change the cache and the UI will automatically update to match the change.

Data is read from the Apollo Cache using GraphQL. You read queries. Data is written to the Apollo Cache using GraphQL, you write data to queries. Consider the `ROOT_QUERY` that is located in `src/App.js`:

```
export const ROOT_QUERY = gql`
    query allUsers {
```

```
            totalUsers
            allUsers { ...userInfo }
            me { ...userInfo }
    }

    fragment userInfo on User {
        githubLogin
        name
        avatar
    }
```

This query has three fields in its selection set: totalUsers, allUsers, and me. We can read any data that we currently have stored in our cache using the cache.readQuery method:

```
let { totalUsers, allUsers, me }  = cache.readQuery({ query: ROOT_QUERY })
```

In this line of code, we've obtained the values for totalUsers, allUsers, and me that were stored in the cache.

We can also write data directly to the totalUsers, allUsers, and me fields of the ROOT_QUERY using the cache.writeQuery method:

```
cache.writeQuery({
    query: ROOT_QUERY,
    data: {
        me: null,
        allUsers: [],
        totalUsers: 0
    }
})
```

In this example, we are clearing all of the data from our cache and resetting default values for all of the fields in the ROOT_QUERY. Because we are using react-apollo, this change would trigger a UI update and clear the entire list of users from the current DOM.

A good place to write data directly to the cache is inside of the logout function in the AuthorizedUser component. At present this function is removing the user's token, but the UI does not update until the "Refetch" button has been clicked or the browser is refreshed. To improve this feature, we will clear out the current user from the cache directly when the user logs out.

First we need to make sure that this component has access to the client in its props. One of the fastest ways to pass this property is to use the withApollo higher order component. This will add the client to the AuthorizedUser component's properties. Since this component already uses the withRouter higher order component, we will use the compose function to make sure that the AuthorizedUser component is wrapped with both higher order components:

```
import { Query, Mutation, withApollo, compose } from 'react-apollo'

class AuthorizedUser extends Component {
    ...
}

export default compose(withApollo, withRouter)(AuthorizedUser)
```

Using compose, we assemble the withApollo and withRouter functions into a single function. withRouter adds the Router's history to the properties, and withApollo adds Apollo Client to the properties.

This means that we can access Apollo Client in our logout method and use it to remove the details about the current user from the cache:

```
logout = () => {
    localStorage.removeItem('token')
    let data = this.props.client.readQuery({ query: ROOT_QUERY })
    data.me = null
    this.props.client.writeQuery({ query: ROOT_QUERY, data })
}
```

The above code not only removes the current user's token from localStorage, it clears the me field for the current user saved in the cache. Now when users log out, they will see the "Sign In with GitHub" button immediately without having to refresh the browser. This button is rendered only when the ROOT_QUERY doesn't have any values for me.

Another place that we can improve our application thorough working directly with the cache is in the src/Users.js file. Currently, when we click the "Add Fake User" button, a mutation is sent to the GraphQL service. The Mutation component that renders the "Add Fake User" button contains the following property:

```
refetchQueries={[{ query: ROOT_QUERY }]}
```

This property tells the client to send an additional query to our service once the mutation has completed. However, we are already receiving a list of the new fake users in the response of the mutation itself:

```
mutation addFakeUsers($count:Int!) {
    addFakeUsers(count:$count) {
        githubLogin
        name
        avatar
    }
}
```

Since we already have a list of the new fake users, there is no need to go back to the server for the same information. What we need to do is obtain this new list of users in the mutation's response and add it directly to the cache. Once the cache changes, the UI will follow.

Find the `Mutation` component in the `Users.js` file that handles the `addFakeUsers` mutation and replace the `refetchQueries` with an `update` property:

```
<Mutation mutation={ADD_FAKE_USERS_MUTATION}
    variables={{ count: 1 }}
    update={updateUserCache}>
    {addFakeUsers =>
        <button onClick={addFakeUsers}>Add Fake User</button>
    }
</Mutation>
```

Now, when the mutation has completed, the response data will be sent to a function called `updateUserCache`:

```
const updateUserCache = (cache, { data:{ addFakeUsers } }) => {
    let data = cache.readQuery({ query: ROOT_QUERY })
    data.totalUsers += addFakeUsers.length
    data.allUsers = [
        ...data.allUsers,
        ...addFakeUsers
    ]
    cache.writeQuery({ query: ROOT_QUERY, data })
}
```

When the `Mutation` component invokes the `updateUserCache` function, it sends the cache and the data that has been returned in the mutation's response.

We want to add the fake users to the current cache, so we'll read the data that is already in the cache using `cache.readQuery({ query: ROOT_QUERY })` and add to it. First, we'll increment the total users, `data.totalUsers += addFakeUsers.length`. Then, we'll concatenate the current list of users with the fake users that we've received from the mutation. Now that the current data has been changed, it can be written back to the cache using `cache.writeQuery({ query: ROOT_QUERY, data })`. Replacing the data in the `cache` will cause the UI to update and display the new fake user.

At this point, we have completed the first version of the User portion of our app. We can list all users, add fake users, and sign in with GitHub. We have built a full stack GraphQL application using Apollo Server and Apollo Client. The `Query` and `Muta tion` components are tools that we can use to quickly begin developing clients with Apollo Client and React.

In Chapter 7, we see how we can incorporate subscriptions and file uploading into the PhotoShare application. We also discuss emerging tools in the GraphQL ecosystem that you can incorporate into your projects.

GraphQL in the Real World

So far, you have designed a schema, constructed a GraphQL API, and implemented a client using Apollo Client. We've taken one complete full-stack iteration with GraphQL and developed an understanding of how GraphQL APIs are consumed by clients. Now it's time to prepare our GraphQL APIs and clients for production.

To take your new skills into production, you are going to need to meet the requirements of your current applications. Our current applications likely allow for file transfer between the client and the server. Our current applications might use WebSockets to push real-time data updates to our clients. Our current APIs are secure and protect against malicious clients. To work with GraphQL in production, we need to be able to meet these requirements.

Also we need to think about our development teams. You might be working with a full-stack team, but more often than not, teams are split into frontend developers and backend developers. How can all of your developers work efficiently from different specializations within our GraphQL stack?

And what about the sheer scope of your current code base? At present, you likely have many different services and APIs running in production and probably have neither the time nor the resources to rebuild everything from the ground up with GraphQL.

In this chapter, we address all of these requirements and concerns. We begin by taking two more iterations in the PhotoShare API. First, we incorporate subscriptions and real-time data transport. Second, we allow users to post photos by implementing a solution for file transport with GraphQL. After we've completed these iterations on the PhotoShare application, we will look at ways to secure our GraphQL API to guard against malicious client queries. We wrap up this chapter by examining ways in which teams can work together to effectively migrate to GraphQL.

Subscriptions

Real-time updates are an essential feature for modern web and mobile applications. The current technology that allows for real-time data transport between websites and mobile applications are WebSockets. You can use the WebSocket protocol to open duplex two-way communication channels over a TCP socket. This means that web pages and applications can send and receive data over a single connection. This technology allows updates to be pushed from the server directly to the web page in real time.

Up to this point, we have implemented GraphQL queries and mutations using the HTTP protocol. HTTP gives us a way to send and receive data between the client and the server, but it does not help us connect to a server and listen for state changes. Before WebSockets were introduced, the only way to listen for state changes on the server was to incrementally send HTTP requests to the server to determine whether anything had changed. We saw how to easily implement polling with the query tag in Chapter 6.

But if we really want to take full advantage of the new web, GraphQL has to be able to support real-time data transport over WebSockets in addition to HTTP requests. The solution is *subscriptions*. Let's take a look at how we can implement subscriptions in GraphQL.

Working with Subscriptions

In GraphQL, you use subscriptions to listen to your API for specific data changes. Apollo Server already supports subscriptions. It wraps a couple of npm packages that are routinely used to set up WebSockets in GraphQL applications: `graphql-subscriptions` and `subscriptions-transport-ws`. The `graphql-subscriptions` package is an npm package that provides an implementation of the publisher/subscriber design pattern, PubSub. `PubSub` is essential for publishing data changes that client subscribers can consume. `subscriptions-transport-ws` is a WebSocket server and client that allows transporting subscriptions over WebSockets. Apollo Server automatically incorporates both of these packages to support subscriptions out of the box.

By default, Apollo Server sets up a WebSocket at `ws://localhost:4000`. If you use the simple server configuration that we demonstrated at the beginning of Chapter 5, you're using a configuration that supports WebSockets out of the box.

Because we are working with `apollo-server-express`, we'll have to take few steps to make subscriptions work. Locate the `index.js` file in the `photo-share-api` and import the `createServer` function from the `http` module:

```
const { createServer } = require('http')
```

Apollo Server will automatically set up subscription support, but to do so, it needs an HTTP server. We'll use `createServer` to create one. Locate the code at the bottom of the `start` function where the GraphQL service is started on a specific port with `app.listen(...)`. Replace this code with the following:

```
const httpServer = createServer(app)
server.installSubscriptionHandlers(httpServer)

httpServer.listen({ port: 4000 }, () =>
    console.log(`GraphQL Server running at localhost:4000${server.graphqlPath}`)
)
```

First, we create a new `httpServer` using the Express app instance. The `httpServer` is ready to handle all of the HTTP requests sent to it based upon our current Express configuration. We also have a server instance where we can add WebSocket support. The next line of code, `server.installSubscriptionHandlers(httpServer)` is what makes the WebSockets work. This is where Apollo Server adds the necessary handlers to support subscriptions with WebSockets. In addition to an HTTP server, our back-end is now ready to receive requests at `ws://localhost:4000/graphql`.

Now that we have a server that is ready to support subscriptions, it's time to implement them.

Posting photos

We want to know when any of our users post a photo. This is a good use case for a subscription. Just like everything else in GraphQL, to implement subscriptions we need to start with the schema first. Let's add a subscription type to the schema just below the definition for the `Mutation` type:

```
type Subscription {
  newPhoto: Photo!
}
```

The `newPhoto` subscription will be used to push data to the client when photos are added. We send a subscription operation with the following GraphQL query language operation:

```
subscription {
    newPhoto {
        url
        category
        postedBy {
            githubLogin
            avatar
        }
    }
}
```

This subscription will push data about new photos to the client. Just like a Query or Mutation, GraphQL allows us to request data about specific fields with selection sets. With this subscription every time there is a new photo, we will receive its url and category along with the githubLogin and avatar of the user who posted this photo.

When a subscription is sent to our service, the connection remains open. It is listening for data changes. Every photo that is added will push data to the subscriber. If you set up a subscription with GraphQL Playground, you will notice that the Play button will change to a red Stop button.

The Stop button means that the subscription is currently open and listening for data. When you press the Stop button, the subscription will be unsubscribed. It will stop listening for data changes.

It is finally time to take a look at the postPhoto mutation: the mutation that adds new photos to the database. We want to publish new photo details to our subscription from this mutation:

```
async postPhoto(root, args, { db, currentUser, pubsub }) {

    if (!currentUser) {
        throw new Error('only an authorized user can post a photo')
    }

    const newPhoto = {
        ...args.input,
        userID: currentUser.githubLogin,
        created: new Date()
    }

    const { insertedIds } = await db.collection('photos').insert(newPhoto)
    newPhoto.id = insertedIds[0]

    pubsub.publish('photo-added', { newPhoto })

    return newPhoto

}
```

This resolver expects that an instance of pubsub has been added to context. We'll do that in the next step. pubsub is a mechanism that can publish events and send data to our subscription resolver. It's like the Node.js EventEmitter. You can use it to publish events and send data to every handler that has subscribed to an event. Here, we publish a photo-added event just after we insert a new photo to the database. The details of the new photo are passed as the second argument of the pubsub.publish method. This will pass details about the new photo to every handler that has subscribed to photo-added events.

Next, let's add the `Subscription` resolver that will be used to subscribe to photo-added events:

```
const resolvers = {

  ...

  Subscription: {
    newPhoto: {
      subscribe: (parent, args, { pubsub }) =>
        pubsub.asyncIterator('photo-added')
    }
  }
}
```

The `Subscription` resolver is a root resolver. It should be added directly to the resolver object right next to the `Query` and `Mutation` resolvers. Within the Subscription resolver, we need to define resolvers for each field. Since we defined the new Photo field in our schema, we need to make sure a `newPhoto` resolver exists in our resolvers.

Unlike `Query` or `Mutation` resolvers, `Subscription` resolvers contain a subscribe method. The subscribe method receives the `parent`, `args`, and `context` just like the any other resolver functions. Inside of this method, we subscribe to specific events. In this case, we are using the `pubsub.asyncIterator` to subscribe to `photo-added` events. Any time a `photo-added` event is raised by `pubsub`, it will be passed through this new photo subscription.

Subscription Resolvers in the Repo

The example files in the GitHub repository breaks the resolvers up into several files. The above code can be found in `resolvers/Subscriptions.js`.

The `postPhoto` resolver and the `newPhoto` subscription resolver both expect there to be an instance of `pubsub` in context. Let's modify the context to include `pubsub`. Locate the `index.js` file and make the following changes:

```
const { ApolloServer, PubSub } = require('apollo-server-express')

...

async function start() {

  ...

  const pubsub = new PubSub()
  const server = new ApolloServer({
```

```
        typeDefs,
        resolvers,
        context: async ({ req, connection }) => {

            const githubToken = req ?
                req.headers.authorization :
                connection.context.Authorization

            const currentUser = await db
                .collection('users')
                .findOne({ githubToken })

            return { db, currentUser, pubsub }

        }
    })

    ...

}
```

First, we need to import the `PubSub` constructor from `apollo-server-express` package. We use this constructor to create a `pubsub` instance and add it to context.

You may have also notice that we change the context function. Queries and mutations will still use HTTP. When we send either of these operations to the GraphQL Service the request argument, `req`, is sent to the context handler. However, when the operation is a Subscription, there is no HTTP request so the `req` argument is `null`. Information for subscriptions is instead passed when the client connects to the WebSocket. In this case, the WebSocket `connection` argument will be sent to the context function instead. When we have a subscription we'll have to pass authorization details through the connection's `context`, not the HTTP request headers.

Now we are ready to try out our new subscription. Open the playground and start a subscription:

```
subscription {
    newPhoto {
        name
        url
        postedBy {
            name
        }
    }
}
```

Once the subscription is running, open a new Playground tab and run the `postPhoto` mutation. Every time you run this mutation, you will see your new photo data sent to the subscription.

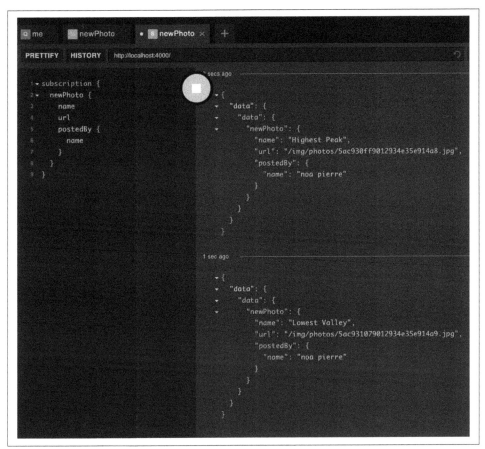

Figure 7-1. The newPhoto subscription in the playground

Challenge: newUser subscription

Can you implement a newUser subscription? Whenever new users are added to the database via the githubLogin or the addFakeUsers mutation, can you publish a *newuser* event to a subscription?

Hint: when handling addFakeUsers, you might need to publish the event a number of times, once for each user added.

If you get stuck, you can find the answer in the repo (*https://github.com/MoonHigh way/learning-graphql/tree/master/chapter-07*).

Consuming Subscriptions

Assuming that you completed the challenge in the preceding sidebar, the PhotoShare server supports subscriptions for Photos and Users. In this next section, we subscribe to the newUser subscription and immediately display any new users on the page. Before we can get started, we need to set up Apollo Client to handle subscriptions.

Adding the WebSocketLink

Subscriptions are used over WebSockets. To enable WebSockets on the server, we need to install a few additional packages:

```
npm install apollo-link-ws apollo-utilities subscription-transport-ws
```

From here, we want to add a WebSocket link to the Apollo Client configuration. Locate the src/index.js file in the photo-share-client project and add the following imports:

```
import {
    InMemoryCache,
    HttpLink,
    ApolloLink,
    ApolloClient,
    split
} from 'apollo-boost'
import { WebSocketLink } from 'apollo-link-ws'
import { getMainDefinition } from 'apollo-utilities'
```

Notice that we've imported split from apollo-boost. We will use this to split GraphQL operations between HTTP requests and WebSockets. If the operation is a mutation or a query, Apollo Client will send an HTTP request. If the operation is a subscription, the client will connect to the WebSocket.

Under the hood of Apollo Client, network requests are managed with ApolloLink. In the current app, this has been responsible for sending HTTP requests to the GraphQL service. Any time we send an operation with the Apollo Client, that operation is sent to an Apollo Link to handle the network request. We can also use an Apollo Link to handle networking over WebSockets.

We'll need to set up two types of links to support WebSockets: an HttpLink and a WebsocketLink:

```
const httpLink = new HttpLink({ uri: 'http://localhost:4000/graphql' })
const wsLink = new WebSocketLink({
    uri: `ws://localhost:4000/graphql`,
    options: { reconnect: true }
})
```

The `httpLink` can be used to send HTTP requests over the network to `http://local host:4000/graphql` and the `wsLink` can be used to connect to `ws://localhost:4000/graphql` and consume data over WebSockets.

Links are composable. That means they can be chained together to build custom pipelines for our GraphQL operations. In addition to being able to send an operation to a single `ApolloLink`, we can send an operation through a chain of reusable links where each link in the chain can manipulate the operation before it reaches the last link in the chain which handles the request and returns a result.

Lets create a link chain with the `httpLink` by adding a custom Apollo Link that is responsible for adding the authorization header to the operation:

```
const authLink = new ApolloLink((operation, forward) => {
    operation.setContext(context => ({
        headers: {
            ...context.headers,
            authorization: localStorage.getItem('token')
        }
    }))
    return forward(operation)
})

const httpAuthLink = authLink.concat(httpLink)
```

The `httpLink` is concatenated to the `authLink` to handle user authorization for HTTP requests. Keep in mind that this `.concat` function is not the same function that you'll find in JavaScript that concatenates arrays. This is a special function that concatenates Apollo Links. Once concatenated, we have more appropriately named the link `httpAuthLink` to describe the behavior more clearly. When an operation is sent to this link, it will first be passed to the `authLink` where the authorization header is added to the operation before it is forwarded to the `httpLink` to handle the network request. If you are familiar with middleware in Express or Redux, the pattern is similar.

Now we need to tell the client which link to use. This is where `split` comes in handy. The `split` function will return one of two Apollo Links based upon a predicate. The first argument of the `split` function is the predicate. A predicate is a function that returns `true` or `false`. The second argument of the split function represents the link to return when the predicate returns `true`, and the third argument represents the link to return when the predicate returns false.

Let's implement a `split` link that will check to see if our operation happens to be a subscriptions. If it is a subscription, we will use the `wsLink` to handle the network, otherwise we will use the `httpLink`:

```
const link = split(
    ({ query }) => {
```

```
            const { kind, operation } = getMainDefinition(query)
            return kind === 'OperationDefinition' && operation === 'subscription'
        },
        wsLink,
        httpAuthLink
    )
```

The first argument is the predicate function. It will check the operation's query AST using the getMainDefinition function. If this operation is a subscription, then our predicate will return true. When the predicate returns true, the link will return the wsLink. When the predicate returns false the link will return the httpAuthLink.

Finally, we need to change our Apollo Client configuration to use our custom links by passing it the link and the cache:

```
    const client = new ApolloClient({ cache, link })
```

Now our client is ready to handle subscriptions. In the next section, we will send our first subscription operation using Apollo Client.

Listening for new users

On the client, we can listen for new users by creating a constant called LIS TEN_FOR_USERS. This contains a string with our subscription that will return a new user's githubLogin, name, and avatar:

```
    const LISTEN_FOR_USERS = gql`
        subscription {
            newUser {
                githubLogin
                name
                avatar
            }
        }
    `
```

Then, we can use the <Subscription /> component to listen for new users:

```
    <Subscription subscription={LISTEN_FOR_USERS}>
        {(({ data, loading }) => loading ?
            <p>loading a new user...</p> :
            <div>
                <img src={data.newUser.avatar} alt="" />
                <h2>{data.newUser.name}</h2>
            </div>
    </Subscription>
```

As you can see here, the <Subscription /> component works like the <Mutation /> or <Query /> components. You send it the subscription, and when a new user is received, their data is passed to a function. The problem with using this component in our app is that the newUser subscription passes one new user at a time. So, the preceding component would show only the last new user that was created.

What we want to do is listen for new users when the PhotoShare client starts, and when we have a new user, we add them to our current local cache. When the cache is updated, the UI will follow, so there is no need to change anything about the UI for new users.

Let's modify the App component. First, we convert it to a class component so that we can take advantage of React's component lifecycle. When the component mounts, we start listening for new users via our subscription. When the App component unmounts, we stop listening by invoking the subscription's unsubscribe method:

```
import { withApollo } from 'react-apollo'

...

class App extends Component {

    componentDidMount() {
        let { client } = this.props
        this.listenForUsers = client
            .subscribe({ query: LISTEN_FOR_USERS })
            .subscribe(({ data:{ newUser } }) => {
                const data = client.readQuery({ query: ROOT_QUERY })
                data.totalUsers += 1
                data.allUsers = [
                    ...data.allUsers,
                    newUser
                ]
                client.writeQuery({ query: ROOT_QUERY, data })
            })
    }

    componentWillUnmount() {
        this.listenForUsers.unsubscribe()
    }

    render() {
        ...
    }
}

export default withApollo(App)
```

When we export the <App /> component, we use the withApollo function to pass the client to the App via props. When the component mounts, we will use the client to start listening for new users. When the component unmounts, we stop the subscription using the unsubscribe method.

The subscription is created using the `client.subscribe().subscribe()`. The first `subscribe` function is an Apollo Client method that is used to send the subscription operation to our service. It returns an observer object. The second `subscribe` function is a method of the observer object. It is used to subscribe handlers to the observer. The handlers are invoked every time the subscription pushes data to the client. In the above code, we've added a handler that captures the information about each new users and adds them directly to the Apollo Cache using `writeQuery`.

Now, when new users are added, they are instantly pushed into our local cache which immediately updates the UI. Because the subscription is adding every new user to the list in real time, there is no longer a need to update the local cache from `src/Users.js`. Within this file, you should remove the `updateUserCache` function as well as the mutation's `update` property. You can see a completed version of the app component at the book's website (*https://github.com/MoonHighway/learning-graphql/tree/master/chapter-07/photo-share-client*).

Uploading Files

There's one last step to creating our PhotoShare application—actually uploading a photo. In order to upload a file with GraphQL, we need to modify both the API and the client so that they can handle `multipart/form-data`, the encoding type that is required to pass a file with a POST body over the internet. We are going to take an additional step that will allow us to pass a file as a GraphQL argument so that the file itself can be handled directly within the resolver.

To help us with this implementation, we are going to use two npm packages: `apollo-upload-client` and `apollo-upload-server`. Both of these packages are designed to pass files from a web browser over HTTP. `apollo-upload-client` will be responsible for capturing the file in the browser and passing it along to the server with the operation. `apollo-upload-server` is designed to handle files passed to the server from `apollo-upload-client`. `apollo-upload-server` captures the file and maps it to the appropriate query argument before sending it to the resolver as an argument.

Handling Uploads on the Server

Apollo Server automatically incorporates the `apollo-upload-server`. There is no need to install that npm in your API project because it's already there and working. The GraphQL API needs to be ready to accept an uploaded file. An `Upload` custom scalar type is provided in the Apollo Server. It can be used to capture the file `stream`, `mimetype`, and `encoding` of an uploaded file.

We'll start with the schema first, adding a custom scalar to our type definitions. In the schema file, we'll add the `Upload` scalar:

```
scalar Upload

input PostPhotoInput {
  name: String!
  category: Photo_Category = PORTRAIT
  description: String,
  file: Upload!
}
```

The Upload type will allow us to pass the contents of a file with our PostPhotoInput.
This means that we will receive the file itself in the resolver. The Upload type contains
information about the file including an upload stream that we can use to save the file.
Let's use this stream in the postPhoto mutation. Add the following code to the bottom of the postPhoto mutation found in resolvers/Mutation.js:

```
const { uploadStream } = require('../lib')
const path = require('path')

...

async postPhoto(root, args, { db, user, pubsub }) => {

    ...

    var toPath = path.join(
        __dirname, '..', 'assets', 'photos', `${photo.id}.jpg`
    )

    await { stream } = args.input.file
    await uploadFile(input.file, toPath)

    pubsub.publish('photo-added', { newPhoto: photo })

    return photo
}
```

In this example, the uploadStream function would return a promise which would be
resolved when the upload is complete. The file argument contains the upload
stream that can be piped to a writeStream and saved locally to the assets/photos
directory. Each newly posted photo will be named based upon its unique identifier.
We are only handling JPEG images in this example for brevity.

If we want to serve these photo files from the same API, we will have to add some
middleware to our Express application that will allow us to serve static JPEG images.
In the index.js file where we set up our Apollo Server, we can add the
express.static middleware that allows us to serve local static files over a route:

```
const path = require('path')

...
```

```
app.use(
    '/img/photos',
    express.static(path.join(__dirname, 'assets', 'photos'))
)
```

This bit of code will handle serving the static files from `assets/photos` to `/img/photos` for HTTP requests.

With that, our server is in place and can now handle photo uploads. It's time to transition to the client side where we'll create a form that can manage photo uploads.

Use a File Service

In a real Node.js application, you would typically save user uploads to a cloud-based file storage service. The previous example uses an `uploadFile` function to upload the file to a local directory, which limits the scalability of this sample application. Services such as AWS, Google Cloud, or Cloudinary can handle large volumes of file uploads from distributed applications.

Posting a New Photo with Apollo Client

Now, let's handle the photos on the client. First to display the photos, we'll need to add the `allPhotos` field to our `ROOT_QUERY`. Modify the following query in the `src/App.js` file:

```
export const ROOT_QUERY = gql`
    query allUsers {
        totalUsers
        totalPhotos
        allUsers { ...userInfo }
        me { ...userInfo }
        allPhotos {
            id
            name
            url
        }
    }

    fragment userInfo on User {
        githubLogin
        name
        avatar
    }
`
```

Now when the website loads, we will receive the `id`, `name`, and `url` of every photo stored in the database. We can use this information to display the photos. Let's create a `Photos` component that will be used to display each photo:

```
import React from 'react'
import { Query } from 'react-apollo'
import { ROOT_QUERY } from './App'

const Photos = () =>
    <Query query={ALL_PHOTOS_QUERY}>
        {(({loading, data}) => loading ?
            <p>loading...</p> :
            data.allPhotos.map(photo =>
                <img
                    key={photo.id}
                    src={photo.url}
                    alt={photo.name}
                    width={350} />

            )
        }
    </Query>

export default Photos
```

Remember, the Query component takes in the ROOT_QUERY as a property. Then, we use the render prop pattern to display all of the photos when loading is complete. For each photo in the data.allPhotos array, we'll add a new img element with metadata that we pull from each photo object including the photo.url and photo.name.

When we add this code to the App component, our photos will be displayed. But first, let's create another component. Let's create a PostPhoto component that will contain the form:

```
import React, { Component } from 'react'

export default class PostPhoto extends Component {

    state = {
        name: '',
        description: '',
        category: 'PORTRAIT',
        file: ''
    }

    postPhoto = (mutation) => {
        console.log('todo: post photo')
        console.log(this.state)
    }

    render() {
        return (
            <form onSubmit={e => e.preventDefault()}
                style={{
                    display: 'flex',
                    flexDirection: 'column',
```

```
                justifyContent: 'flex-start',
                alignItems: 'flex-start'
            }}>

            <h1>Post a Photo</h1>

            <input type="text"
                style={{ margin: '10px' }}
                placeholder="photo name..."
                value={this.state.name}
                onChange={(({target}) =>
                    this.setState({ name: target.value })} />

            <textarea type="text"
                style={{ margin: '10px' }}
                placeholder="photo description..."
                value={this.state.description}
                onChange={(({target}) =>
                    this.setState({ description: target.value })} />

            <select value={this.state.category}
                style={{ margin: '10px' }}
                onChange={(({target}) =>
                    this.setState({ category: target.value })}>
                <option value="PORTRAIT">PORTRAIT</option>
                <option value="LANDSCAPE">LANDSCAPE</option>
                <option value="ACTION">ACTION</option>
                <option value="GRAPHIC">GRAPHIC</option>
            </select>

            <input type="file"
                style={{ margin: '10px' }}
                accept="image/jpeg"
                onChange={(({target}) =>
                    this.setState({
                        file: target.files && target.files.length ?
                            target.files[0] :
                            ''
                    })} />

            <div style={{ margin: '10px' }}>
                <button onClick={() => this.postPhoto()}>
                    Post Photo
                </button>
                <button onClick={() => this.props.history.goBack()}>
                    Cancel
                </button>
            </div>

        </form>
    )
}
```

```
}
```

The `PostPhoto` component is simply a form. This form uses input elements for the `name`, `description`, `category`, and the `file` itself. In React, we call this controlled because each input element is linked to a state variable. Any time an input's value changes, the state of the `PostPhoto` component will change too.

We submit photos by pressing the "Post Photo" button. The file input accepts a JPEG and sets the state for `file`. This state field represents the actual file, not just text. We have not added any form validation to this component for brevity.

It's time to add our new components to the `App` component. When we do so, we will make sure that the home route displays our `Users` and `Photos`. We will also add a `/newPhoto` route that can be used to display the form.

```
import React, { Fragment } from 'react'
import { Switch, Route, BrowserRouter } from 'react-router-dom'
import Users from './Users'
import Photos from './Photos'
import PostPhoto from './PostPhoto'
import AuthorizedUser from './AuthorizedUser'

const App = () =>
    <BrowserRouter>
        <Switch>
            <Route
                exact
                path="/"
                component={() =>
                    <Fragment>
                        <AuthorizedUser />
                        <Users />
                        <Photos />
                    </Fragment>
                } />
            <Route path="/newPhoto" component={PostPhoto} />
            <Route component={({ location }) =>
                <h1>"{location.pathname}" not found</h1>
            } />
        </Switch>
    </BrowserRouter>

export default App
```

The `<Switch>` component allows us to render one route at a time. When the url contains the home route, "/", we will display a component that contains the `Authorize dUser`, `Users`, and `Photos` components. The `Fragment` is used in React when we want to display sibling components without having to wrap them in an extra `div` element. When the route is "/newPhoto", we will display the new photo form. And when the route is not recognized, we will display a h1 element that let's the user know that we can't find the route that they provided.

Only authorized users can post photos, so we'll append a "Post Photo" NavLink to the AuthorizedUser component. Clicking this button will cause the PostPhoto to render.

```
import { withRouter, NavLink } from 'react-router-dom'

...

class AuthorizedUser extends Component {

    ...

    render() {
        return (
            <Query query={ME_QUERY}>
                {(({ loading, data }) => data.me ?
                    <div>
                        <img
                            src={data.me.avatar_url}
                            width={48}
                            height={48}
                            alt="" />
                        <h1>{data.me.name}</h1>
                        <button onClick={this.logout}>logout</button>
                        <NavLink to="/newPhoto">Post Photo</NavLink>
                    </div> :
                </div> :

        ...
```

Here we import the <NavLink> component. When the Post Photo link is clicked, the user will be sent to the /newPhoto route.

At this point, the app navigation should work. A user is allowed to navigate between screens, and when posting a photo, we should see the necessary input data logged in the console. It is time for us to take that post data, including the file, and send it with a mutation.

First, let's install apollo-upload-client:

```
npm install apollo-upload-client
```

We are going to replace the current HTTP link with an HTTP link that is supplied by apollo-upload-client. This link will support multipart/form-data requests that contain upload files. To create this link, we'll use the createUploadLink function:

```
import { createUploadLink } from 'apollo-upload-client'

...

const httpLink = createUploadLink({
```

```
        uri: 'http://localhost:4000/graphql'
    })
```

We've replaced the old HTTP link with a new one called using the `createUploadLink` function. This looks fairly similar to the HTTP link. It has the API route included as the `uri`.

It's time to add the `postPhoto` mutation to the `PostPhoto` form:

```
import React, { Component } from 'react'
import { Mutation } from 'react-apollo'
import { gql } from 'apollo-boost'
import { ROOT_QUERY } from './App'

const POST_PHOTO_MUTATION = gql`
    mutation postPhoto($input: PostPhotoInput!) {
        postPhoto(input:$input) {
            id
            name
            url
        }
    }
`
```

The `POST_PHOTO_MUTATION` is our mutation parsed as an AST and ready to be sent to the server. We import the `ALL_PHOTOS_QUERY` because we'll need to use it when it is time to update the local cache with the new photo that will be returned by the mutation.

To add the mutation, we will encapsulate the Post Photo button element with the `Mutation` component:

```
<div style={{ margin: '10px' }}>
    <Mutation mutation={POST_PHOTO_MUTATION}
        update={updatePhotos}>
        {mutation =>
            <button onClick={() => this.postPhoto(mutation)}>
                Post Photo
            </button>
        }
    </Mutation>
    <button onClick={() => this.props.history.goBack()}>
        Cancel
    </button>
</div>
```

The Mutation component passes the mutation as a function. When we click the button, we will pass the mutation function to `postPhoto` so that it can be used to change the photo data. Once the mutation is complete, the `updatePhotos` function will be called in order to update the local cache.

Next, let's actually send the mutation:

```
postPhoto = async (mutation) => {
    await mutation({
        variables: {
            input: this.state
        }
    }).catch(console.error)
    this.props.history.replace('/')
}
```

This mutation function returns a promise. Once complete, we will use React Router to navigate the user back to the home page by replacing the current route using the history property. When the mutation is complete, we need to capture the data returned from it to update the local cache:

```
const updatePhotos = (cache, { data:{ postPhoto } }) => {
    var data = cache.readQuery({ query: ALL_PHOTOS_QUERY })
    data.allPhotos = [
        postPhoto,
        ...allPhotos
    ]
    cache.writeQuery({ query: ALL_PHOTOS_QUERY, data })
}
```

The `updatePhotos` method handles the cache update. We will read the photos from the cache using the `ROOT_QUERY`. Then, we'll add the new photo to the cache using `writeQuery`. This little bit of maintenance will make sure that our local data is in sync.

At this point, we are ready to post new photos. Go ahead and give it a shot.

We've taken a closer look at how queries, mutations, and subscriptions are handled on the client side. When you're using React Apollo, you can take advantage of the `<Query>`, `<Mutation>`, and `<Subscription>` components to help you connect the data from your GraphQL service to your user interface.

Now that the application is working, we'll add one more layer to handle security.

Security

Your GraphQL service provides a lot of freedom and flexibility to your clients. They have the flexibility to query data from multiple sources in a single request. They also have the ability to request large amounts of related, or connected, data in a single request. Left unchecked, your clients have the capability of requesting too much from your service in a single request. Not only will the strain of large queries affect server performance, it could also take your service down entirely. Some clients might do this unwittingly or unintentionally, whereas other clients might have more malicious intent. Either way, you need to put some safeguards in place and monitor your server's performance in order to protect against large or malicious queries.

In this next section, we cover some of the options available to improve the security of your GraphQL service.

Request Timeouts

A *request timeout* is a first defense against large or malicious queries. A request timeout allows only a certain amount of time to process each request. This means that requests of your service need to be completed within a specific time frame. Request timeouts are used not only for GraphQL services, they are used for all sorts of services and processes across the internet. You might have already implemented these timeouts for your Representational State Transfer (REST) API to guard against lengthy requests with too much POST data.

You can add an overall request timeout to the express server by setting the `timeout` key. In the following, we've added a timeout of five seconds to guard against troublesome queries:

```
const httpServer = createServer(app)
server.installSubscriptionHandlers(httpServer)

httpServer.timeout = 5000
```

Additionally, you can set timeouts for overall queries or individual resolvers. The trick to implementing timeouts for queries or resolvers is to save the start time for each query or resolver and validate it against your preferred timeout. You can record the start time for each request in context:

```
const context = async ({ request }) => {

    ...

    return {
        ...
        timestamp: performance.now()
    }

}
```

Now each of the resolvers will know when the query began and can throw an error if the query takes too long.

Data Limitations

Another simple safeguard that you can place against large or malicious queries is to limit the amount of data that can be returned by each query. You can return a specific number of records, or a page of data, by allowing your queries to specify how many records to return.

For example, recall in Chapter 4 that we designed a schema that could handle data paging. But what if a client requested an extremely large page of data? Here's an example of a client doing just that:

```
query allPhotos {
  allPhotos(first=99999) {
    name
    url
    postedBy {
        name
        avatar
    }
  }
}
```

You can guard against these types of large requests by simply setting a limit for a page of data. For example, you could set a limit for 100 photos per query in your GraphQL server. That limit can be enforced in the query resolver by checking an argument:

```
allPhotos: (root, data, context) {
    if (data.first > 100) {
        throw new Error('Only 100 photos can be requested at a time')
    }
}
```

When you have a large number of records that can be requested, it is always a good idea to implement data paging. You can implement data paging simply by providing the number of records that should be returned by a query.

Limiting Query Depth

One of the benefits GraphQL provides the client is the ability to query connected data. For example, in our photo API, we can write a query that can deliver information about a photo, who posted it, and all the other photos posted by that photograph all in one request:

```
query getPhoto($id:ID!) {
    Photo(id:$id) {
        name
        url
        postedBy {
            name
            avatar
            postedPhotos {
                name
                url
            }
        }
    }
}
```

This is a really nice feature that can improve network performance within your applications. We can say that the preceding query has a depth of 3 because it queries the photo itself along with two connected fields: `postedBy` and `postedPhotos`. The root query has a depth of 0, the `Photo` field has a depth of 1, the `postedBy` field has a depth of 2 and the `postedPhotos` field has a depth of 3.

Clients can take advantage of this feature. Consider the following query:

```
query getPhoto($id:ID!) {
    Photo(id:$id) {
        name
        url
        postedBy {
            name
            avatar
            postedPhotos {
                name
                url
                taggedUsers {
                    name
                    avatar
                    postedPhotos {
                        name
                        url
                    }
                }
            }
        }
    }
}
```

We've added two more levels to this query's depth: the `taggedUsers` in all of the photos posted by the photographer of the original photo, and the `postedPhotos` of all of the `taggedUsers` in all of the photos posted by the photographer of the original photo. This means that if I posted the original photo, this query would also resolve to all of the photos I've posted, all of the users tagged in those photos, and all of the photos posted by all of those tagged users. That's a lot of data to request. It is also a lot of work to be performed by your resolvers. Query depth grows exponentially and can easily get out of hand.

You can implement a query depth limit for your GraphQL services to prevent deep queries from taking your service down. If we had set a query depth limit of 3, the first query would have been within the limit, whereas the second query would not because it has a query depth of 5.

Query depth limitations are typically implemented by parsing the query's AST and determining how deeply nested the selection sets are within these objects. There are npm packages like `graphql-depth-limit` that can assist with this task:

```
npm install graphql-depth-limit
```

After you install it, you can add a validation rule to your GraphQL server configuration using the depthLimit function:

```
const depthLimit = require('graphql-depth-limit')

...

const server = new ApolloServer({
    typeDefs,
    resolvers,
    validationRules: [depthLimit(5)],
    context: async({ req, connection }) => {
        ...
    }
})
```

Here, we have set the query depth limit to 10, which means that we provided our clients with the capability of writing queries that can go 10 selection sets deep. If they go any deeper, the GraphQL server will prevent the query from executing and return an error.

Limiting Query Complexity

Another measurement that can help you identify troublesome queries is *query complexity*. There are some client queries that might not run too deep but can still be expensive due to the amount of fields that are queried. Consider this query:

```
query everything($id:ID!) {
  totalUsers
  Photo(id:$id) {
    name
    url
  }
  allUsers {
    id
    name
    avatar
    postedPhotos {
      name
      url
    }
    inPhotos {
      name
      url
      taggedUsers {
        id
      }
    }
  }
}
```

The everything query does not exceed our query depth limit, but it's still pretty expensive due to the number of fields that are being queried. Remember, each field maps to a resolver function that needs to be invoked.

Query complexity assigns a complexity value to each field and then totals the overall complexity of any query. You can set an overall limit that defines the maximum complexity available for any given query. When implementing query complexity you can identify your expensive resolvers and give those fields a higher complexity value.

There are several npm packages available to assist with the implementation of query complexity limits. Let's take a look at how we could implement query complexity in our service using graphql-validation-complexity:

```
npm install graphql-validation-complexity
```

GraphQL validation complexity has a set of default rules out of the box for determining query complexity. It assigns a value of 1 to each scalar field. If that field is in a list, it multiplies the value by a factor of 10.

For example, let's look at how graphql-validation-complexity would score the everything query:

```
query everything($id:ID!) {
  totalUsers        # complexity 1
  Photo(id:$id) {
    name            # complexity 1
    url             # complexity 1
  }
  allUsers {
    id              # complexity 10
    name            # complexity 10
    avatar          # complexity 10
    postedPhotos {
      name          # complexity 100
      url           # complexity 100
    }
    inPhotos {
      name          # complexity 100
      url           # complexity 100
      taggedUsers {
        id          # complexity 1000
      }
    }
  }
}                   # total complexity 1433
```

By default, graphql-validation-complexity assigns each field a value. It multiplies that value by a factor of 10 for any list. In this example, totalUsers represents a single integer field and is assigned a complexity of 1. Querying fields in a single photo have the same value. Notice that the fields queried in the allUsers list are assigned a value of 10. This is because they are within a list. Every list field is multiplied by 10. So a list within a list is assigned a value of 100. Because `taggedUsers` is a list within the `inPhotos` list, which is within the `allUsers` list, the values of taggedUser fields is $10 \times 10 \times 10$, or 1000.

We can prevent this particular query from executing by setting an overall query complexity limit of 1000:

```
const { createComplexityLimitRule } = require('graphql-validation-complexity')

...

    const options = {

        ...

        validationRules: [
            depthLimit(5),
            createComplexityLimitRule(1000, {
                onCost: cost => console.log('query cost: ', cost)
            })
        ]
    }
```

In this example, we set the maximum complexity limit to 1000 with the use of the `createComplexityLimitRule` found in the `graphql-validation-complexity` package. We've also implemented the `onCost` function, which will be invoked with the total cost of each query as soon as it is calculated. The preceding query would not be allowed to execute under these circumstances because it exceeds a maximum complexity of 1000.

Most query complexity packages allow you to set your own rules. We could change the complexity values assigned to scalars, objects, and lists with the `graphql-validation-complexity` package. It is also possible to set custom complexity values for any field that we deem very complicated or expensive.

Apollo Engine

It is not recommended to simply implement security features and hope for the best. Any good security and performance strategy needs metrics. You need a way to monitor your GraphQL service so that you can identify your popular queries and see where your performance bottlenecks occur.

You can use *Apollo Engine* to monitor your GraphQL service, but it's more than just a monitoring tool. Apollo Engine is a robust cloud service that provides insights into your GraphQL layer so that you can run the service in production with confidence. It monitors the GraphQL operations sent to your services and provides a detailed live report available online at *https://engine.apollographql.com*, which you can use to identify your most popular queries, monitor execution time, monitor errors, and help find bottlenecks. It also provides tools for schema management including validation.

Apollo Engine is already included in your Apollo Server 2.0 implementation. With just one line of code, you can run Engine anywhere that Apollo Server runs, including serverless environments and on the edge. All you need to do is turn it on by setting the `engine` key to `true`:

```
const server = new ApolloServer({
    typeDefs,
    resolvers,
    engine: true
})
```

The next step is to make sure that you have an environment variable called `ENGINE_API_KEY` set to your Apollo Engine API key. Head to *https://engine.apollog raphql.com* to create an account and generate your key.

In order to publish your application to Apollo Engine, you will need to install the Apollo CLI tools:

```
npm install -g apollo
```

Once installed you can use the CLI to publish your app:

```
apollo schema:publish
    --key=<YOUR ENGINE API KEY>
    --endpoint=http://localhost:4000/graphql
```

Don't forget to add your `ENGINE_API_KEY` to the environment variables as well.

Now when we run the PhotoShare GraphQL API, all operations sent to the GraphQL service will be monitored. You can view an activity report at the Engine website. This activity report can be used to help find and alleviate bottlenecks. Additionally, Apollo Engine will improve the performance and response time of our queries as well as monitor the performance of our service.

Taking the Next Steps

Throughout this book, you've learned about graph theory; you've written queries; you've designed schemas; you've set up GraphQL servers and explored GraphQL client solutions. The foundation is in place, so you can use what you need to improve your applications with GraphQL. In this section, we share some concepts and resources that will further support your future GraphQL applications.

Incremental Migration

Our PhotoShare app is a prime example of a Greenfield project. When you are working on your own projects, you might not have the luxury of starting from scratch. The flexibility of GraphQL allows you to start incorporating GraphQL incrementally. There's no reason that you need to tear down everything and start over to benefit from GraphQL's features. You can start slow by applying the following ideas:

Fetch data from REST in your resolvers
> Instead of rebuilding every REST endpoint, use GraphQL as a gateway and make a fetch request for that data on the server inside of a resolver. Your service can also cache the data sent from REST to improve query response time.

Or use GraphQL request
> Robust client solutions are great, but implementing them at the start might be too much setup. To get started simply, use `graphql-request` and make a request in the same place you use `fetch` for a REST API. This approach will get you started, get you hooked on GraphQL, and will likely lead you to a more comprehensive client solution when you're ready to optimize for performance. There is no reason you cannot fetch data from four REST endpoints and one GraphQL service within the same app. Everything does not have to migrate to GraphQL all at the same time.

Incorporate GraphQL in one or two components
> Instead of rebuilding your entire site, pick a single component or page and drive the data to that particular feature using GraphQL. Keep everything else about your site in place while you monitor the experience of moving a single component.

Don't build any more REST endpoints
> Instead of expanding REST, build a GraphQL endpoint for your new service or feature. You can host a GraphQL endpoint on the same server as your REST endpoints. Express does not care if it is routing a request to a REST function or a GraphQL resolver. Every time a task requires a new REST endpoint, add that feature to your GraphQL service, instead.

Don't maintain your current REST endpoints
> The next time there is a task to modify a REST endpoint or create a custom endpoint for some data, don't! Instead, take the time to section off this one endpoint and update it to GraphQL. You can slowly move your entire REST API this way.

Moving to GraphQL slowly can allow you to benefit from features right away without the pains associated with starting from nothing. Start with what you have, and you can make your transition to GraphQL a smooth and gradual one.

Schema-First Development

You're at a meeting for a new web project. Members of different frontend and backend teams are represented. After the meeting, someone might come up with some specifications, but these documents are often lengthy and underutilized. Frontend and backend teams start coding, and without clear guidelines, the project is delivered behind schedule and is different than everyone's initial expectations.

Problems with web projects usually stem from a lack of communication or miscommunication about what should be built. Schemas provide clarity and communication, which is why many projects practice *schema-first development*. Instead of getting bogged down by domain-specific implementation details, disparate teams can work together on solidifying a schema before building anything.

Schemas are an agreement between the frontend and the backend teams and define all of the data relationships for an application. When teams sign off on a schema, they can work independently to fulfill the schema. Working to serve the schema yields better results because there is clarity in type definitions. Frontend teams know exactly which queries to make to load data into user interfaces. Backend teams know exactly what the data needs are and how to support them. Schema-first development provides a clear blueprint, and the teams can build the project with more consensus and less stress.

Mocking is an important part of Schema First Development. Once the front-end team has the schema, they can use it to start developing components immediately. The following code is all that is needed to stand up a mock GraphQL service running on `http://localhost:4000`.

```
const { ApolloServer } = require('apollo-server')
const { readFileSync } = require('fs')

var typeDefs = readFileSync('./typeDefs.graphql', 'UTF-8')

const server = new ApolloServer({ typeDefs, mocks: true })

server.listen()
```

Assuming you've provided the `typeDefs.graphql` file designed during the schema-first process, you can begin developing UI components that send query, mutation, and subscription operations to the mock GraphQL service while the back-end team implements the real service.

Mocks work out of the box by providing default values for each scalar type. Everywhere a field is supposed to resolve to a string, you'll see "Hello World" as the data.

You can customize the data this is returned by a mock server. This makes it possible to return data that looks more like the real data. This is an important feature that will assist with the task of styling your user interface components:

```
const { ApolloServer, MockList } = require('apollo-server')
const { readFileSync } = require('fs')

const typeDefs = readFileSync('./typeDefs.graphql', 'UTF-8')
```

```
const resolvers = {}

const mocks = {
  Query: () => ({
    totalPhotos: () => 42,
    allPhotos: () => new MockList([5, 10]),
    Photo: () => ({
      name: 'sample photo',
      description: null
    })
  })
}

const server = new ApolloServer({
  typeDefs,
  resolvers,
  mocks
})

server.listen({ port: 4000 }, () =>
  console.log(`Mock Photo Share GraphQL Service`)
)
```

The above code adds a mock for the `totalPhotos` and `allPhotos` fields along with the `Photo` type. Every time we query the `totalPhotos` the number 42 will be returned. When we query the `allPhotos` field we will receive somewhere between 5 and 10 photos. The `MockList` constructor is included in the `apollo-server` and is used to generate list types with specific lengths. Every time a `Photo` type is resolved by the service the `name` of the photo is "a sample photo" and the description is `null`. You can create pretty robust mocks in conjunction with packages like `faker` or `casual`. These npms provide all sorts of fake data that can be used to build realistic mocks.

To learn more about mocking an Apollo Server, check out Apollo's documentation (*https://www.apollographql.com/docs/apollo-server/v2/features/mocking.html*).

GraphQL Events

There are a number of conferences and meetups that focus on GraphQL content.

GraphQL Summit (https://summit.graphql.com/)
    A conference organized by Apollo GraphQL.

GraphQL Day (https://www.graphqlday.org/)
    A hands-on developer conference in The Netherlands.

GraphQL Europe (https://www.graphql-europe.org/)
    A nonprofit GraphQL conference in Europe.

GraphQL Finland (https://graphql-finland.fi/)
    A community-organized GraphQL conference in Helsinki, Finland.

You'll also find GraphQL content at almost any development conference, particularly those that focus on JavaScript.

If you're looking for events near you, there are also GraphQL meetups in cities all over the world (*http://bit.ly/2lnBMB0*). If there's not one near you, you could be the one to start a local group!

Community

GraphQL is popular because it's a wonderful technology. It also is popular due to the fervent support of the GraphQL community. The community is quite welcoming, and there are a number of ways of getting involved and staying on top of the latest changes.

The knowledge that you've gained about GraphQL will serve as a good foundation when you're exploring other libraries and tools. If you're looking to take the next steps to expand your skills, here are some other topics to check out:

Schema stitching
    Schema stitching allows you to create a single GraphQL schema from multiple GraphQL APIs. Apollo provides some great tooling around the composition of remote schemas. Learn more about how to take on a project like this in the Apollo documentation (*http://bit.ly/2KcibP6*).

Prisma
    Throughout the book, we've used GraphQL Playground and GraphQL Request: two tools from the Prisma team. Prisma is a tool that turns your existing database into a GraphQL API, no matter what database you're using. While a GraphQL API stands between the client and the database, Prisma stands between a GraphQL API and the database. Prisma is open-source, so you can deploy your Prisma service in production using any cloud provider.

    The team has also released a related tool called Prisma Cloud, a hosting platform for Prisma services. Instead of having to set up your own hosting, you can use Prisma Cloud to manage all of the DevOps concerns for you.

AWS AppSync
    Another new player in the ecosystem is Amazon Web Services. It has released a new product built on GraphQL and Apollo tools to simplify the process of setting up a GraphQL service. With AppSync, you create a schema and then connect to your data source. AppSync updates the data in real-time and even handles offline data changes.

Community Slack Channels

Another great way to get involved is to join one of the many GraphQL community Slack channels. Not only can you stay connected to the latest news in GraphQL, but you can ask questions sometimes answered by the creators of these technologies.

You can also share your knowledge with others in these growing communities from wherever you are:

- GraphQL Slack (*https://graphql-slack.herokuapp.com/*)
- Apollo Slack (*https://www.apollographql.com/#slack*)

As you continue your journey with GraphQL, you can become more involved in the community as a contributor, as well. Right now, there are high-profile projects like React Apollo, Prisma, and GraphQL itself that have open issues with help wanted tags. Your help with one of these issues could help many others! There are also many opportunities to contribute new tools to the ecosystem.

Though change is inevitable, the ground under our feet as GraphQL API developers is very solid. At the heart of everything we do, we're creating a schema and writing resolvers to fulfill the data requirements of the schema. No matter how many tools come out to shake things up in the ecosystem, we can rely on the stability of the query language itself. On the API timeline, GraphQL is very new, but the future is very bright. So, let's all go build something amazing.

Index

Symbols

! (exclamation point), 60

A

abstract syntax trees, 53-55
access token, 112
adjacent nodes, 22
Amazon Web Services (AWS), 179
API tools, 33-38
    GraphiQL, 33-36
    GraphQL Playground, 36-38
    public GraphQL APIs, 38
API, GraphQL
    client setup, 123-128
    context, 104-107
    creating, 83-121
    fetch requests, 123-125
    GitHub authorization, 107-121
    graphql-request, 125-128
    monitoring, 174-175
    resolvers, 84-101
Apollo Client, 128
    about, 13
    and cache, 128
    Mutation component, 135
    posting a new photo with, 162-168
    project setup, 129
    Query component, 131
    WebSocket link, 156
Apollo Engine, 174-175
Apollo Server, 150
apollo-server-express, GraphQL, 102
AppSync, 179
arguments, 68-72

    data paging, 70
    defined, 41
    filtering, 69-72
    organizing with input types, 74-77
    sorting, 71
authentication, 115-121
    fake users mutation, 119-121
    me query, 115-117
authorization
    client-side, 137
    GitHub, 107-121
    identifying the user, 141
    of user, 137
AWS AppSync, 179

B

Bad Credentials error, 115
Berners-Lee, Tim, 1
binary trees, 26
Byron, Lee, 6

C

cache, Apollo Client and, 128
clients, 12, 123
    (see also Apollo Client)
    authorization, 137
    fetch requests, 123-125
    graphql-request, 125-128
    using a GraphQL API, 123-128
Codd, Edgar M., 31
community, 179-180
    GraphQL events, 178
    Slack channels, 180
connections

many-to-many, 64, 96-97
one-to-many, 62, 93-96
one-to-one, 61
queries and, 41
resolvers and, 93-97
schemas and, 60-68
context, 104-107
adding database to, 105
defined, 104
MongoDB installation for, 104
create-react-app, 129
Crockford, Douglas, 7
cURL, 33, 123-125
custom scalars, 97-101

D

data paging, 70
data transport, history of, 6
declarative data-fetching language, 4
definitions, in GraphQL Document, 54
degree of a node, 22
depth of a node, 25
design principles, GraphQL, 5
directed graph (digraph)
defined, 20
Twitter as, 28
documentation, of schemas, 79-81

E

edges (term), 18
endpoints, managing, 11
enums (enumeration types), 59, 91-92
error handling, 39
Euler, Leonhard, 21-24
Eulerian cycle, 23
Eulerian path, 23
exclamation point, 60
Express
and Node.js, 102

F

Facebook
and GraphQL's origins, 5
as undirected graph, 27
subscriptions and, 51
SWAPI project, 38
fake users mutation, 119-121
fetch requests, 123-125

Fielding, Roy, 7
fields, 58
filtering, 69-72
data paging, 70
sorting, 71
FragmentDefinition, 54
fragments
and union types, 46
interfaces, 47
queries and, 43-48

G

GitHub API, 38
GitHub authorization, 107-121
authenticating users, 115-121
Bad Credentials error, 115
fake users mutation, 119-121
githubAuth mutation, 112-115
me query, 115-117
postPhoto mutation, 117
process of, 111
setting up GitHub OAuth, 108-110
GitHub OAuth
return types, 77
setting up, 108-110
GitHub, as early adopter of GraphQL, 12
graph theory, 15-30
history of, 20-24
real-world applications of concepts, 27-30
real-world examples of graphs, 15-17
trees as graphs, 24-27
vocabulary of, 18-20
GraphiQL, 33-36
GraphQL (generally)
about, 1-13
and history of data transport, 6
basics, 2-5
clients, 12
design principles, 5
origins, 5
real world uses, 12
specification, 4
GraphQL Bin, 37
GraphQL Day, 178
GraphQL Europe, 178
GraphQL Finland, 179
GraphQL Playground, 36-38, 115
GraphQL Summit, 178
graphql-request, 125-128

H

Homebrew, 105
HTML trees, 26

I

incremental migration, 175
inline fragments, 47
input types
    with resolvers, 91-92
    with schemas, 74-77
input variables, 50
interfaces, 47, 67
introspection, 52

J

JSON (JavaScript Object Notation), origins of, 7

K

Königsberg bridge problem, 20-24

L

lexical analysis (lexing), 53
lists
    and interfaces, 67
    of different types, 66-68
    schemas and, 60-68
    union types, 46, 66

M

many-to-many connections, 64, 96-97
me query, 115-117
migration, incremental, 175
MongoDB, installing, 104
monitoring, API, 174-175
Mutation component, 135
mutations, 48-50
    about, 32
    and query variables, 50
    declaring variables, 74
    defining in the schema, 72-74
    fake user, 119-121
    githubAuth, 112-115
    postPhoto, 117

N

nodes
    adjacent, 22

    defined, 18
    degree of, 22
non-nullable fields
    defined, 58
    exclamation points and, 60
nullable fields, 58

O

object types (see types)
one-to-many connections, 42, 62, 93-96
one-to-one connections, 61
OperationDefinition, 54
operations, defined, 34
overfetching, 8-9

P

parent object, 91
PhotoShare application
    GraphQL API for, 83-121
    GraphQL clients for, 123
    schema design, 57-81
    security, 168-175
    subscriptions, 150-160
    uploading files, 160-168
Playground (see GraphQL Playground)
Prisma, 179
public GraphQL APIs, 38
PubSub, 150

Q

query arguments, 41
query complexity, 172-174
Query component, 131
query document, 34
query language, 31-55
    abstract syntax trees, 53-55
    API tools, 33-38
    edges and connections, 41
    fragments, 43-48
    introspection, 52
    mutations, 48-50
    simple GraphQL query example, 32
    subscriptions, 51
query variables, 50
query(ies)
    as GraphQL root type, 40
    data limitations on, 169
    defined, 38

error handling, 39
limiting complexity of, 172-174
limiting depth of, 170-172
simple GraphQL example, 32

R

React Router, 137
React, Apollo Client with, 129
real-world applications of GraphQL, 149-180
incremental migration, 175
schema-first development, 176
security, 168-175
subscriptions, 150-160
uploading files, 160-168
Relay, 13
request timeouts, 169
resolvers
custom scalars, 97-101
defined, 84
edges and connections, 93-97
githubAuth, 113
root, 86-88
type, 88-91
using inputs and enums, 91-92
REST (Representational State Transfer), 7-12
basic data operations, 31
drawbacks, 7-12
managing endpoints, 11
origins, 7
overfetching, 8-9
underfetching, 9-11
return types, 77
root nodes, 24
root resolvers, 86-88
root type, 40
RPC (remote procedure call), 6

S

scalar types, 59
custom scalars, 97-101
defined, 41
enums, 59
Schafer, Dan, 6
Schema Definition Language (SDL), 57
Schema First design methodology, 57, 176
schema stitching, 179
schemas
arguments, 68-72
connections and lists, 60-68

defined, 57
designing, 57-81
documentation, 79-81
input types, 74-77
mutations, 72-74
return types, 77
subscription types, 78
types, 57-60
Schrock, Nick, 6
security, 168-175
API monitoring, 174-175
data limitations on queries, 169
limiting query complexity, 172-174
limiting query depth, 170-172
request timeouts, 169
selection sets, 40
SelectionSet, 54
servers, GraphQL
handling uploads on, 160
Slack channels, 180
SOAP (Simple Object Access Protocol), 6
social authorization, 107
sorting, 71
specification (spec), 4
SQL (Structured Query Language), 31-55
state changes (see mutations, subscriptions)
subscriptions, 51
and WebSocketLink, 156
consuming, 156-160
in schemas, 78
listening for new users, 158-160
posting photos, 151
real-world applications, 150-160
working with, 150-155
subtrees, 26
SWAPI (Star Wars API), 38

T

tagging, 64
through types, 64
timeouts, request, 169
trees
abstract syntax trees, 53-55
as graphs, 24-27
trivial resolvers, 90
Twitter, as directed graph, 28
type resolvers, 88-91
types, 41
basics, 58

defining, 57-60
enums, 59
in GraphQL, 58
interfaces, 47, 67
lists of different types, 66-68
scalar, 59
through, 64
union, 46, 66

U

underfetching, 9-11
undirected graph
    defined, 19
    Facebook as, 27
union types, 46, 66
uploading files, 160-168
    handling uploads on the server, 160

posting a new photo with Apollo, 162-168

V

variables
    input, 50
    mutation, 74
vertices (term), 18

W

WebSocketLink, 156
WebSockets, 150
WorldWideWeb, origins of, 1

Y

Yelp GraphQL API, 38

About the Authors

Alex Banks and **Eve Porcello** are software engineers and instructors based in Tahoe City, California. With their company, Moon Highway, they have developed and delivered custom training curriculum for corporate clients and online for LinkedIn Learning. They also are the authors of *Learning React* from O'Reilly Media.

Colophon

The animal on the cover of *Learning GraphQL* is Bonelli's Eagle (*Aquila fasciata*). This large raptor is found across Southeast Asia, the Middle East, and the Mediterranean, preferring drier climates and areas where it can nest in crags or tall trees. It has an average wingspan of about 60 in., and it is distinguished by a dark-brown head and wings with a white underbelly adorned in dark stripes and flecks.

Usually silent outside of the nest, this stealthy hunter feeds primarily on other birds, up to and including other raptors, but is also known to eat small mammals and reptiles. Despite a propensity to eat other birds of prey, adult nesting pairs are known for their affection for chicks regardless of lineage, and have been observed to foster eggs and hatchlings in abandoned nests, both of *Aquila fasciata* and other raptor species in which lethal aggression is not displayed between siblings.

Many of the animals on O'Reilly covers are endangered; all of them are important to the world. To learn more about how you can help, go to animals.oreilly.com.

The cover image is from *Brehms Tierleben*. The cover fonts are URW Typewriter and Guardian Sans. The text font is Adobe Minion Pro; the heading font is Adobe Myriad Condensed; and the code font is Dalton Maag's Ubuntu Mono.

O'REILLY®

There's much more where this came from.

Experience books, videos, live online training courses, and more from O'Reilly and our 200+ partners—all in one place.

Learn more at oreilly.com/online-learning

9 781492 030713